A PLEA FOR
EVANGELICAL
DEMONSTRATION

For twenty-five years American Christians have eagerly read what Dr. Carl F. H. Henry has to say The religion editor of United Press International singles him out as "probably the most noted evangelical theologian in the United States." He was founding editor of **Christianity Today,** and is currently professor-at-large at Eastern Baptist Theological Seminary and visiting professor of theology at Trinity Evangelical Divinity School. A respected educator and lecturer, he is author of eighteen books. He received the B.A. and M.A. degrees from Wheaton College, B.D. and Th D. from Northern Baptist Theological Seminary, and Ph.D. from Boston University.

A PLEA FOR EVANGELICAL DEMONSTRATION

by Carl F. H. Henry

BAKER BOOK HOUSE
Grand Rapids, Michigan

Library of Congress Catalog Card Number: 78-159778
Standard Book Number: 8010-4019-1

Quotations from *The New English Bible* (NEB)
© the Delegates of the Oxford University Press,
and the Syndics of the Cambridge University Press 1961, 1970.
Reprinted by permission.

PRINTED IN THE UNITED STATES OF AMERICA

Dr. Henry's Other Books on Ethics

The Uneasy Conscience of Modern Fundamentalism (1947)
Christian Personal Ethics (1957)
Aspects of Christian Social Ethics (1964)

Preface

M any hundreds of students, Christian ministers, and professors have publicly applauded the lectures contained in this book, and share my conviction that this very message today needs urgently to "get through." I have decided, therefore, to release them for publication under the indicated title so their main point will not be lost. The lectures voice an agonizing concern over the unsure fortunes of our evangelical witness in the closing decades of this century, and bear on the need of effective evangelical engagement.

These essays assume that the social crisis today has reached proportions so acute that some problems at least are sufficiently urgent that Christian moral protest has become imperative. Even where evangelicals may not be wholly sure which alternative specifics they prefer, they are not exempt from indicating wholly unacceptable policies and practises, and the risk of achieving only a modest improvement of a bad situation is better than total loss through silence.

If Bible-believing Christians can wade against the secular stream by mass evangelistic crusades aimed to rescue otherwise doomed sinners, they can summon enough courage and concern in public — at least, I am convinced they can, and will, if fully aroused to the urgency of these times — to stand against the culture in majestic witness to the holy commandments of God.

In opening remarks as chairman of the World Congress on Evangelism (Berlin, 1966), I emphasized to Christian participants from more than one hundred lands that justice and justification are concerns of equal importance to God: "The God of the Bible is the God of justice and of justification. The Christian evangelist has a message doubly relevant to the modern scene; he knows that *justice* is due to all because a just God created mankind in his holy image, and he knows that all men need *justification* because the Holy Creator sees us as rebellious sinners. The gospel is good news, not simply because it reinforces modern man's lost sense of personal worth and confirms the demand for universal justice on the basis of creation, but also because it offers rebellious men as doomed sinners that justification and redemption without which no man can see God and live" *(One Race, One Gospel, One Task,* Carl F. H. Henry and W. Stanley Mooneyham, eds., Minneapolis: World Wide Publications, 1967, p. 16).

The evangelical community has carried the burden for evangelism more surely than it has carried the burden for social justice. Regional and national congresses in many parts of the world have followed the World Congress on Evangelism to implement the missionary task; I have myself shared in such ventures in Singapore, Yugoslavia, and Canada. At the evangelistic frontiers of every land and every city in the world much remains to be done; I can only plead for a widening and deepening of evangelistic commitments.

But continuing neglect of the evangelical social witness will be a tragic and costly mistake. Its penalties will surely include the restriction of the very evangelistic witness on which Bible-believing Christians concentrate. Wherever nations are given over to unjust rulers that is the inevitable prospect; their tyrannical policies impede religious freedom, cloud the supremacy of God's commands, and retard the public proclamation of the message of Christ. But the need to emphasize social justice is urgent not alone where dictatorial tyrants loom on the horizon. Even where religious liberty prevails and Christ is openly preached amidst the cultural upheavals of our time, the public power of evangelism itself is seriously curtailed wherever God's will for society is not known, and men addressed as sinners do not fully comprehend what they need to be justified from or to what righteousness they need to be restored. If the misimpression thrives that Christian commitment has significance only for internal and private life, secular multitudes who now sense how urgent the world crisis is, and how serious are our social problems, will simply turn elsewhere for seeming solutions that cannot but promise more than they can actually provide.

In order not to keep the reader standing longer at the front door, let me invite him to move into the various articles that supply the chapters of this book, pausing only to hang each essay on its proper hook.

The first chapter, "A Plea for Evangelical Demonstration," was welcomed by *Christian Herald,* and expanded somewhat without altering its original emphasis at the invitation of Editor Kenneth Wilson. It appeared in that publication early in 1971.

"Christian Theology and Social Change" was presented in shorter, extemporaneous form at Perkins School of Theology, Southern Methodist University, in 1967. A reprint of that seminary lecture appeared under the title "Christian Theology and Social Revolution" in *The Perkins School of Theology Journal,* Vol. XXI, Numbers 2 and 3, Winter-Spring 1967-68.

"The Theology of Evangelism" was delivered to the Canadian Congress on Evangelism in Ottawa, 1970. It was also given as a public lecture sponsored in Singapore by the Disciples' Training Center.

"The Theology of Revolution" is an address delivered at Moody Bible Institute in October, 1970, and at Eastern Mennonite College in February, 1971.

"Personal Evangelism and Social Justice" was delivered

as one of the Ryan Lectures at Asbury Theological Seminary in September, 1970, and repeated at Moody Bible Institute. It was also given at the Michigan Methodist Ministers Conference in August, 1970, and at Pacific Lutheran University in March, 1971.

"The Truth of the Gospel" was delivered to the Canadian Congress on Evangelism at Ottawa in 1970.

CARL F. H. HENRY

Easter, 1971

Contents

A Plea for 1
Evangelical Demonstration

This is a call for authentic evangelical protest.

A sensitive Christian conscience must openly confront enduring and intractable social injustices. Biblically-concerned Christians need not forego a moment of open identification with those of other faiths and alien views in protesting what all together recognize to be unjust.

The one mistake evangelicals dare not make, however, is to dilute their witness into merely a mood and mentality of protest, that is, to extend their moment of identification into a day and generation of protest. The Old Testament prophets not only entered actively into the social milieu, but they also fearlessly proclaimed God's articulate Word. Their understanding of social protest was bracketed by the revealed will of God. They made known the commandments of God.

To get underway, evangelical demonstration requires a cadre of concerned persons willing to be publicly identified in active, vocal confrontation, and within a covering strategy that contemplates in advance the possible courses of action in the eventuality of failure or success. It requires using audio-visual imagery to dramatize group engagement through the mass media, enlisting all available evangelical talent in a cooperative and coordinated thrust.

These preparatory factors, to be sure, by no means guar-

antee an authentically evangelical witness. Something more
is needed.

Evangelicals know that injustice is reprehensible not
simply because it is anti-human but because it is anti-God.
Evangelicals are pro-God, pro-Christ, in their fundamental
commitment. Visibility and audibility for God's commands
are therefore indispensable to evangelical engagement. To
proclaim "Thou shalt not . . ." and what "the Bible says"
as specifically as possible is an evangelical imperative.
Evangelicals must make God's Word and ways known because it is the divine will and demand that is flouted
by social injustice.

Evangelical declaration of God's Word need not today
be couched in ancient verbiage. Familiar formulas too
often register upon the modern spirit like dull clichés. The
truth of God can be stated as effectively and sometimes
much more so in modern language and idiom than in King
James English. But the principles thus proclaimed must
be Biblical if the message is to be authentically Christian.
Despite the knowledge explosion of our times few people
today — churchgoers included — seem to know what God
wills, what Scripture says, and what Jesus taught.

That the Crucified and Risen Jesus will return to judge the
world for its unrighteousness was an essential part of apostolic preaching. Yet more is expected of Christians than
simply warning the world that nations march off the map,
societies sink into chaos, and men are destined for hell if
they scrap the commandments of God.

The air must vibrate with the joy of obedience to God's
commands — with freedom-songs, with truth-lyrics, with
holiness-and-happiness motifs that reflect the spiritual liberty
wrought by God through forgiveness and renewal. Evangelicals ought to be matching song and melody to a social
witness.

Why do evangelicals leave to the Roman Catholic Church
the high contribution of a socially-relevant *Hymnal for*

Young Christians? If through the singing of freedom songs the Selma marchers could rally courage to protest social wrongs in the face of hostility and danger, surely new hymns of holy liberty and godly joy should be able to rally sluggard evangelical loyalties.

Evangelical college students should be encouraged to echo the good news of a better prospect and way in the open arenas of life. Why shouldn't glee clubs and supportive bands set student bodies marching not simply in a massive public crusade against social injustice — necessary as that moment of indictment is — but also in a corporate witness for the cause of God in the world? It is a hopeful sign that a younger generation of evangelical Christians is beginning to see the need for larger evangelical demonstration. They know that the social struggle cannot be won by bumper stickers.

While the opportunity still remains Christian educators had best buy up student involvement on evangelical premises. Unless evangelical colleges set socially-concerned students in motion under a Biblical banner, students who cannot live with a stifled social conscience will become active under other flags. Many evangelical students are seething with impatience over the lack of aggressive involvement for social change and are eager for social engagement. Unless authentic evangelical opportunities are charted, this cresting determination can take misguided and highly unfortunate directions.

On evangelical campuses social concern has largely been channeled into social service. This is a desirable outlet, but it is not enough. Social critique is an authentic part of evangelical mission.

On secular campuses the evangelical student vanguard has been trapped in the dilemma whether to be counted with radical forces devoted to nebulous alternatives and interested mainly in disrupting the existing structures, or to stand on the sidelines and seem socially insensitive, when in some instances authentic issues of social justice have been at stake. Dramatic evangelical opportunities have been forfeited in a university environment which all too often deals with basic issues in a predominantly relativistic way. Campus uprisings against authority, rampant problems of sexual immorality and drug addiction, prevalence of practical atheism and indifference to spiritual concerns are not unrelated to the academic stance on life that the universities themselves inculcate. Yet many of our prestigious American colleges were called into being with a Christian intention now all but evaporated. Why then do not radical demonstrations provide a high opportunity for evangelical counter-demonstrations in which students themselves raise the right questions for public education: Has education killed God? Are moral absolutes passé? Is truth a mere bias? Is Jesus a four-letter word?

Evangelicals need to break through their tardiness and timidity on public moral issues and identify frontier concerns while, as Editor Kenneth L. Wilson of the *Christian Herald* puts it, they "are still coming up and are only the size of a man's hand. Why cannot church people routinely take the lead in discovering what the moral issues are? Why must the Church wait until the Supreme Court defines the issues (as in race relations), or until the Church is put in the position of merely reacting to somebody else's initiative?"

Were Ralph Nader an evangelical Protestant we might afford ourselves the luxury of self-congratulation over courageous concern about pollution. Young people are asking whether, after thousands of years of opportunity for planetary development, this generation will leave unfit for human survival the only planet on which we know human life to be possible. Is that not a cause for evangelical initiative?

Had evangelical Protestants contributed Charles Malik to the arena of international concerns we might compliment ourselves over courageous involvement in world political conflict. Young people today are asking whether, after six thousand years of civilization, evangelicals will merely sit in the bleachers as spectators or merely share in the slaughter while the polarized nations move ever closer to a devastating nuclear war that could erase the last vestiges of human civilization. Is that no cause for evangelical concern?

The vision of a new creation and a new society ought not to be forfeited — least of all by Christians — to those who are enamored of short-shrift utopian ideologies. The Bible is a declaration of emancipation; we are sub-evangelical if we feel uneasy over Jesus' deliberate use of the passage from Isaiah: "He has sent me to announce good news to the poor, . . . to let the broken victims go free, to proclaim the year of the Lord's favour" (Luke 4:18, New English Bible). One need not fill God's New Covenant with modern sociopolitical ideals to retain and repeat its challenge to modern politico-economic injustices.

If it really wants to register its witness on the masses, the evangelical vanguard must look beyond mere expectation of newspaper coverage or television comment on its newly-ventured social involvement. A word-and-witness task force must move beyond street placards and press quotes to register convictions in letters to the editors, in tracts and pamphlets, in public addresses and sermons, in interpretative essays and magazine articles, and set public protest in the context of an evangelical response to the truth and demands of God. The common core and hub of such a witness will be the God of justice and of justification, the God who demands the right and who offers new life and joy for doing it.

The most distinctive phase of evangelical involvement comes, therefore, at the level of foundational principle and interpretation. Because liberal and radical movements lack any really convicing rationale for their absolutes, they can justify neither their positions nor the limits of their engagement, whether of escalation or de-escalation. In their one-sided commitment to evolutionary development many liberal Protestants now empty the doctrine of creation into an inner existential relationship of spiritual dependence and forfeit any clear emphasis on God's external causal creation of the world and man. But a merely evolutionary doctrine of origins can supply no basis for universal and enduring human rights. Not for universal human rights, because some Hitler may always arise to contend that in the evolutionary development of mankind one strand (in Hitler's estimate, the Jews) is inferior to the others. Not for enduring human rights, because, as Bertrand Russell saw, if man has emerged from primal protozoa then someday a species of supra-human life may evolve from whose standpoint humanity as we now know it will appear as insignificant as protozoa now appear to contemporary man.

The realm of evangelical expertise in social morality should be to identify why a situation is wrong, when and why it demands public confrontation, and precisely what the right alternative is. It is a glaring weakness of ecumenical social action groups that they so frequently urge changes in civil law — most recently in respect to abortion — without clarifying on Biblical grounds the line between right and wrong.

This does not imply, however, that evangelicals are free to opt out of social involvement when it comes to public identification at the point of actual presence and protest, and to let others go it alone in applying moral pressure to effect needed social change. It means, rather, that evangelicals will engage not simply for the sake of demonstration, nor for the sake of revolution.

Surely one need not have evangelical loyalties in order to publicly denounce discrimination against minorities in the face of legal assurances of equality. But it would certainly reflect a shallow feeling for justice if Christians, who have always been a minority, protested injustice only when some of their own number were the object of discrimination. Not only does the Christian know as a member of the family of mankind that every human being deserves equality before the law, but he knows additionally as a Christian that the living God wills government to preserve justice for all. And as a Christian he had best remember that a government which discriminates against minorities may sooner or later discriminate against the Christian minority.

The Christian not only has liberty to protest flagrant social injustices publicly, but he has in fact a double basis, his humanity and his religious vision, for applying fearless moral pressure against unjust power pockets.

The evangelical is free to participate with non-evangelicals in the moment of protest because his common humanity no less than his religious vision motivates him. He has a special additional duty, however, of correlating such participation with his comprehensive philosophy and strategy of Christian concern and commitment, to which any and every tactical maneuver of evangelical protest must be related. Social engagement can never for the evangelical be merely a matter of sticking one's nose into a one-shot pressure group, the sole enduring evidence of personal participation being the group photograph in tonight's newspaper. It involves, rather, a putting-on-the-line of a life that is God's, a readiness, if need be, to be battered and bruised for Christ's sake — as the holy men who faced jeers and flogging, fetters and prison bars, were stoned, tortured to death, and even sawn in two (Heb. 11:35 ff.).

Because one need not be an evangelical to share in public protest is no excuse for evangelicals to elaborate their distinctives only outside and beyond the moment of common involvement, and not within the moment of protest itself. It may be especially imperative, in fact, that evangelicals somehow maintain their distinctiveness at the very instant of common protest, no less than in the preceding and subsequent hours of deliberation and interpretation.

The moment of protest is today often set within a strategy

pursued by social radicals who in the interest of revolutionary alternatives are in conflict with all inherited institutional
structures. In such cases where a revolutionary group tries
to muster social discontent for dubious objectives, Christians
will find no common cause.

Christians should avoid hurrying to the point of public
protest in a manner that implies despair over democratic
processes or neglects personal efforts for social change. If
Christians move hurriedly to the point of protest against
the existing system, without patiently probing the possibilities of change through the established structures of government, they imply that the system itself is corrupt and create
needless sympathy for revolutionary forces bent mainly on
destroying the system.

In the moment of protest the evangelical engages not as
the incarnation of righteousness but as one who knows that
all men — protesting and protested alike — are sinners. He
knows that the right is not what the protesters enunciate,
but rather what God wills. He knows why what is protested
is wrong; he knows that little is gained for social stability
by combating the wrong for wrong reasons or by condoning
some flagrant wrongs while concentrating on one among
many. It becomes obvious that the evangelical needs to give
clear visibility to the command and word of God at the
point of protest.

One way for evangelicals to be marked off from others
is to determine for themselves when and how they will join
in the moment of common protest and when and how they
will regroup. Church bells might ring at the precise moment
of evangelical participation, and even summon concerned
believers to open identification. Or evangelicals could con-
ceivably wear an identifying armband, perhaps of green as
a symbol of hope for a better day (rather than of black to
mourn the present), or they might adopt some other equally
simple alternative that the hawkers of gimmicks cannot
commercially exploit. Best of all would be their distinctive

faith-and-freedom songs, their matching of hope and holiness to music, and their united visible witness to the word of God and the command of God. In this way the moment of protest in social criticism becomes a transition to the context of witness in hope. Hosannas and hallelujahs are far more powerful than any impersonal symbol, especially so if evangelical concerns in social affairs are coordinated with evangelical concerns in prayer meetings both in the churches and in neighborhood cell groups. "Thy will be done on earth as it is in heaven" thus becomes, as Jesus intended, a matter of Christian self-yearning, and not merely a placard for publicly condemning others. Such interpersonal spiritual relationships, moreover, sometimes inspire decisions that can alter social conditions far more effectively and impressively than can public pressure.

There is another course, however, that would enable evangelicals to dispense with the need specially to distinguish themselves even at the point of public protest. Representing as it does the largest segment of American Protestantism, the evangelical community could rise boldly to serve the God of justice and of justification in new devotion to evangelism and social justice. In that event evangelicals would hold the center of action in the thrust for the national good. Other forces interested only in a segment of what God wants in public affairs would be left with the burden of explaining why they have ventured into a moment of common identification within an evangelical initiative and context, or would be left with the embarrassment of explaining why they had opted out.

Evangelicals must not wait for liberals and humanitarians to define the issues of injustice and then to usurp the field of action. Rather, evangelicals must learn to set the issues and even to initiate protest when lesser alternatives have failed and intolerable grievances persist.

Twenty years ago I wrote *The Uneasy Conscience of Modern Fundamentalism*. Two decades is long enough for growing up. More recently Sherwood Wirt, editor of *Decision*, has written *The Social Conscience of the Evangelical*. The time is overdue for a dedicated vanguard to move evangelical witness to frontier involvement in the social crisis, an involvement to be followed, pray God, by universal engagement of the evangelical churches in social witness and betterment. Too long have evangelicals acted as if protest were proper only when directed against the liberals and their mistakes. It is high time the minority reached its majority and maturity.

Christian Theology 2
and Social Change

$\mathbf{A}$ merican Protestant orthodoxy has produced no unified social ethics or program of evangelical social action. Some of its scholars have long investigated such concerns, and a few have projected a comprehensive ethic that elaborates God's moral claim upon church and world into a framework of principles, policies, and programs.

But the interpretation of public and social concerns in America has been pre-empted largely by liberal and neo-Protestant writers, who have maintained initiative and influence in the field despite their promotion of successive and competitive theories characterized by repeated revision. The influence of the liberal seminaries, particularly of Union Theological Seminary in New York where for decades some faculty members eagerly correlated Christian ethics with socialist theory, and then of interlocking denominational and ecumenical boards through which liberal churchmen registered their views upon affiliated churches and upon men in public life, are among the most formative factors in explaining the rise of what is now widely viewed as the Protestant social ethic.

I.

It would be too simplistic, however, to say that evangelical Protestant indifference, and forfeiture of an aggressive

23

social role, led to the present non-evangelical or neo-Protestant misunderstanding of the nature and direction of the church's proper role in society. The evangelical community did indeed squander an effective opportunity to articulate the public relevance of the Bible at a time when the American social scene was in ferment. It may be said, however, that more was done by way of an evangelical social witness than most neo-Protestants think.

Lack of communication and significant dialogue between non-evangelical and evangelical forces is a characteristic feature of the past forty years of American religious life. One of the ironies of the ecumenical movement is that it progressively hardened the lines of discourse between the advocates of Biblical Christianity and the proponents of a new theology. This barrier is as formidable today as it was a generation ago. The atmosphere of cold war hangs as low over much of the dialogue between neo-Protestant ecumenical leaders and evangelicals inside the conciliar movement as between those leaders and evangelicals outside the National Council of Churches. This is due largely to the political realities of the religious scene, and to the neo-Protestant use of religious power to dilute evangelical institutions; it is due in part also to the tendency of certain fundamentalist polemicists to attack personalities rather than to criticize ideas and practices.

It should be noted, however, that evangelical Protestantism produced competent internal and external criticisms of the theology of classic modernism, of neo-orthodoxy, and of existentialism; on the American scene, a succession of able scholars since J. Gresham Machen's day has formulated the claim of orthodox Christianity *vis-a-vis* the contemporary alternatives. Yet except for a small but significant company of chastened liberals, most neo-Protestants have been disinterested in returning to a thoroughly Biblical theology; in fact, the ecumenical milieu and ecumenical seminaries today

seldom give even marginal visibility to evangelical perspectives, while both anti-evangelical and non-Protestant scholars
are honored with lecture series, faculty posts, and required
reading. There is no reason to think, therefore, that the
exposition of a unified and comprehensive social ethic by
evangelical Protestants in America would have inverted the
neo-Protestant trend. Instead, the probabilities are that in
the present climate of ecumenical activism a principled
evangelical social ethic would have been ignored as fully
as evangelical theology. The ecclesiastical power structures
have been and are dominated by proponents of neo-Protestant perspectives that consciously advocate novel frontier
approaches.

Nonetheless evangelical failure to elaborate a schematic
social ethic is a blemish on the record of that religious community to which, more than any other, America owes its
distinctive heritage. The influence of evangelical Christian
convictions is unmistakable in the early American political
documents with their emphasis on man's rights and duties,
the limits of government power, and the suspension of revolution upon the prior exhaustion of every means of persuasion. Few can doubt that it is evangelical revivalism that,
at frequent intervals from the days of the frontier circuit
riders to the modern mass crusades of Evangelist Billy
Graham, has renewed the moral will and religious spirit of
the American masses. Until the present generation, when
the Puritan ethic has come under conspicuous attack during
a time of widespread ethical laxity, the characterizing virtues
of American life were largely shaped by Biblical ideals.
Even in decades of moral decline, those ideals have remained
for vast numbers of citizens identified with the churches
the ultimate standards by which to judge human conduct.
Given this identification with the nation's cultural heritage,
a religious movement whose doctrinally-conservative clergy
and laymen represented the convictions of a large and decisive majority of American Protestants ought to have shared

this writer's disturbance, voiced in *The Uneasy Conscience
of Modern Fundamentalism* (1947). The concern expressed
there was that evangelical ethical perspectives consisted too
largely only of an emphasis on personal piety and of a
reactionary protest against objectionable incursions into the
public order of self-assertive neo-Protestants in the name of
institutional Christianity.

Whatever might have been the neo-Protestant response
to an evangelical witness, evangelical Christianity was not
exempt from a spiritual duty to formulate its own positions
positively and coherently, for guiding its own community
of faith. In the absence of a comprehensive formulation,
the misunderstanding grew that evangelical commitment
implies Christian indifference in public affairs; laymen in
the churches took mainly an anti-liberal stance on socio-
political issues without comprehending the overall social
relevance of the Biblical revelation. Meantime, in their
search for a schematic understanding of social ethics, young
intellectuals in colleges and seminaries were abandoned to
liberal teachers and writers.

This situation was nothing less than tragic for evangelical
Christianity in the present generation, and the long roots
of what happened are to be found in the fundamentalist
miscarriage of the evangelical-modernist theological controversy. Necessary as was the condemnation and repudiation of modernism (even Karl Barth later called it "heresy"),
the fundamentalist test of belief served more effectively as
a device to expose the theological unbelief and verbal ambiguity of the liberal scholars than as an adequate framework
for projecting a full-orbed Scriptural theology. In these
circumstances even some neo-orthodox scholars were left
to fill a theological vacuum — which they did from their
own dialectical perspective — that fundamentalism was per-
petuating. In social ethics the situation was similar. In
the larger denominations a non-evangelical leadership that
espoused modern social theories and advanced contro-

versial positions in cooperation with the Federal Council of Churches, and then the National Council of Churches, placed evangelical forces on the defensive. The debatable positions were aggressively propagandized through the mass media, and the church-related educational institutions were increasingly staffed to conform and support the newer theories. The American Council of Christian Churches and the National Association of Evangelicals rallied independent and interdenominational churches for a theological and social witness *over against* the neo-Protestant conciliar stance.

But evangelical Christians could and should also have been instructed in a comprehensive grasp of the Scriptural alternative, and of the alien contra-Biblical assumptions that underlie the neo-Protestant views. This orientation would indeed have supplied a sounder basis for Christian commitment in the public arena than simply to leave social concerns mainly to reaction against the neo-Protestant initiative, however inevitable this was because of the ecumenical establishment's increasing intrusion into the political order as the authentic voice of American Christianity. A coherent understanding of the Biblical ethic, in its social as well as personal relevance, would have prepared the evangelical churches for an effective witness in the time of public confusion that must inevitably attend the collapse of the latest neo-Protestant innovations.

The failure of non-evangelical reconstructions of Christian social duty is inevitable, as evangelical Christians insist, because they rest on a falsification of the real world and a misunderstanding of man and history. Why then did evangelical Christianity concentrate its energies mainly in repudiating the non-evangelical deviations, instead of expounding social ethics on Scriptural presuppositions? One fact is sure. The evangelical churches were not now, as in the fundamentalist era a generation ago, motivated by confidence in the Lord's imminent return; within such an expectation a social witness may seem far less important than concentrating all resources upon evangelism. Today many evangelical leaders who are thoroughly committed to evangelism as the primary task of the Church affirm the need also of a social witness. They sense that even the Christian Church's evangelistic opportunities on the American scene have been seriously impaired because an entire generation has passed in which evangelical Christianity has largely withdrawn from the public arena. They do not think that confidence in the Lord's imminent return reduces social engagement to a needless waste of evangelical energies.

Yet in respect to evangelical polemics it must be emphasized that hostility to neo-Protestant formulations of a supposedly Christian ethic rested upon sound Biblical instinct. The present disruption of American Christianity, with its sharp cleavages inside and outside the conciliar movement, can be understood only in terms of a powerful ecumenical hierarchy's repeated efforts to establish within conciliar Protestantism a quasi-official non-evangelical theology and non-evangelical social ethic. Only an overview of the novel perspectives that undergird institutional Protestant commitments in the twentieth century will indicate why evangelical Christians, bound by a loyalty to the Scriptures, considered the repudiation of the positions advanced in the name of the Church of Jesus Christ a prime spiritual duty.

II.

Neo-Protestant social ethics in America has taken three main forms: (1) The Social Gospel, predicated on the immanental theology of classic modernism; (2) The Niebuhrian Ethic, predicated broadly on the dialectical theology of neo-orthodoxy; and (3) The Ethic of Social Revolution, predicated on an existential and secular theology.

A. *The Social Gospel: Classic Modernism*

The gradual social incarnation of God was the central theme of the Social Gospel, which relied on the Hegelian theory of intensive divine immanence and for its ideological supports on the Darwinian theory of progressive natural evolution. Both emphases were invoked to subvert the historic Christian assertion of transcendent divine redemption (on which the Social Gospel's early spokesman, Walter Rauschenbusch [1861-1918], insisted over against optimistic views of human nature). In its influential form, the Social Gospel regarded neither the bent of man's nature nor his corporate activities nor the social structures as an obstacle to the progressive manifestation of the Kingdom of God. As the means for extending the Kingdom it projected a universal *love*-ethic, supposedly predicated on the example and teaching of Jesus. Man's nature was held to be responsive to reason, educable to love, and perfectible, because essentially good. The state was considered mainly as a corporate extension of individual relationships; justice was defined as a form of benevolence, so that the state reflects and assists in the gradual spiritualization of history. Since the state in the Social Gospel was not considered an agent of justice in distinction from love, its role was viewed as essentially benevolent (defined on socialist premises), pacifism was advocated and capital punishment was assailed.

The Federal Council of the Churches of Christ was formed in 1908, when the Social Gospel was already a formative influence, and through the organization of social action agencies in the leading Protestant denominations it contributed to its further popularity. Although World War I tempered its optimism, it continued to furnish the main framework for ecumenical social thought and action, and left a permanent mark upon many American churches.

The theological and moral weaknesses of the Social Gospel were unmasked by large numbers of American evangelicals, and perhaps by none more lucidly than by J. Gresham Machen (1881-1937). But American ecumenism was already consciously committed to theological pluralism and to ecumenical inclusivism; many of its leaders were zealously promoting theological liberalism and the Social Gospel. So high a priority was given ecumenical inclusivism that Machen's writings were simply ignored by some church leaders who viewed him as ecclesiastically controversial, and scholars in ecumenically-unaffiliated churches were simply disregarded. Meanwhile leaders in the Federal Council of Churches so aggressively espoused their non-evangelical positions, and advocated elements of socialist theory and controversial economic policies, that counter-ecumenical movements arose in the form of the American Council of Christian Churches (1940) and the National Association of Evangelicals (1941). These agencies have continued in a competitive position alongside the National Council of Churches, which in 1950 succeeded the Federal Council of Churches as the official interdenominational organization of twenty-five Protestant denominations and four Eastern Orthodox bodies.

The influx of neo-orthodox theology from Germany and the rise of World War II challenged confidence in education and science and greatly contained its creative force. National Council spokesmen in this period moderated Social Gospel expectations that the Kingdom of God would come on earth in the near future. But they did not relax advocacy of politico-economic policies in the name of Christ and advancement of specific legislative goals as official ecclesiastical objectives in the public arena.

B. *The Niebuhrian Ethic: Dialectical Theology*

The collapse of the theology of divine immanence, with its expectation of the social incarnation of God through socio-economic changes in man's environment, did not lead to an American rediscovery of the orthodox Protestant view of the relevance of Christianity to the social problems of our age. Evangelical ethics had shown its social power in eighteenth century Britain, and has been widely credited with having saved England from the adverse consequences of the French Revolution; and in the Netherlands, in the forepart of this century, Abraham Kuyper had effectively stressed the relevance of an ethic of revelation for all realms of life. The orthodox critique cut across the Social Gospel by emphasizing the transcendence as well as immanence of God, man's corruption of the divine order of creation through his fall and the downward bent of human nature and history, and God's purpose to preserve justice in a fallen society through civil government. It emphasized as well the unique redemptive mission of the church and its indispensable offer of new life in Christ, the proclamation of the revealed moral principles by which society must live if civilization is to endure, and the witness and example of Christian citizens working in the public order for maximal justice.

It was Reinhold Niebuhr, however, who became the influential social theologian in American neo-Protestantism's shift from nineteenth century liberal perspectives to a social ethic predicated on critical insights into the nature of man and history. The transition from the Social Gospel to Niebuhrian ethics marked at one and the same time a perpetuation of the revolt against historic evangelical ethics and a continuance of many of the socio-economic emphases spawned by the Social Gospel. In his early years Niebuhr had shared the semi-humanistic religious liberalism and social idealism of the modernist era, but experience with the actualities of social life and reflection on the drift of world history drove him toward a more realistic view. In *Moral Man and Immoral Society* (1932) he combined an emphasis on corruptive selfishness in the individual and in the corporate structures of life with a social radicalism that bordered on Marxism. Although World War II later moderated Niebuhr's enthusiasm for socialism, his doctrine of man's fall and sinfulness and of the ambiguities of history was forged on an anti-evangelical base, and his social con-

cern worked itself out practically in many pro-socialist
commitments. In his Gifford Lectures, *The Nature and Destiny of Man* (1941-43), he restated the Augustinian-Refor-
mation view of man in the context of a dialectical and
existential analysis of the human situation.

In rejecting the modernist expectation of the social incarnation of God, Niebuhr specifically disowns the miraculous
supernaturalism of Judeo-Christian revealed religion, and
discards the Biblical view of the primal creation of a moral
man whose subsequent fall involves the whole human race
in corruption, guilt, and penalty. While he emphasizes, as
do the Scriptures, God's transcendence and man's selfishness,
Niebuhr nonetheless elaborates these tenets in the context
of a permanent dialectical tension between the eternal and
the historical. The ambiguities of man's creaturely existence
and the corruption of his egocentricity are such that he
inevitably sins; corporate man, moreover, is less moral than
man acting individually. The social structures, therefore,
are not responsive to the love-ethic, which is inadequate due
to the moral tension and ambiguity of history, and must be
reinforced by power that promotes justice. Human nature
is so perverse, says Niebuhr, that neither moral nor rational
suasion will restrain human beings from selfishly exploiting
each other; without the restraints of government to check
men's evil lusts by the use of power in a sinful world, society
would be reduced to anarchy. But the perils of collective
power are also legion; the collective ego represented by the
state must not be given totalitarian exemption from divine
judgment.

Niebuhr therefore proposes a social ethic that formulates
the relationship between love and justice in the context of
dialectical tension between the eternal and temporal. Although morally inferior to either a moral and rational
form of collective cohesion, or the community of love,
the only realistic expedient in society is the promotion of
justice by the use of power; any other estimate of man and

the social process is victimized by illusions. In *Moral Man and Immoral Society* Niebuhr asserted that the principle of coercion necessarily voids pacifism as a perfectionist form that is inapplicable to political life; later he characterized nonviolent resistance as a type of social irresponsibility.

Yet Niebuhr asserts that *agape* is the law of our life and that the relation between time and eternity is adequately expressed only through the paradox of grace. The ultimate ethical referent is the perfect love revealed in the cross of Christ, or radical self-giving. Thus he poses the problem of the relation of Christ to historical forms of power: Christ as the norm of love is final, but the norm is beyond history. Nonetheless world brotherhood remains as a regulative definition of our creative possibilities, and men must strive for what remains a historical impossibility. "There is no escape from the paradoxical relation of history to the Kingdom of God. History moves toward the realization of the Kingdom but yet the judgment of God is upon every new realization" (*Human Destiny*, p. 286).

Niebuhrian ethics reasserted divine transcendence and human sinfulness, the inadequacy of *agape* social ethics and the indispensability of the state's coercive role in preserving order and justice in fallen society, and emphasized the limitations of a purely rationalistic approach to the problems of human life and destiny. Niebuhr formulated his views, however, not in the context of the ontological categories of Biblical Christianity, which he rejected, but rather in terms of subjective categories of his own, and in an existential framework of theology unfamiliar to the Biblical writers, although he frequently appeals to the Biblical view in a manner that undeservedly attaches the prestige of the profoundest of all religions to his ethical theory. As a result, the Niebuhrian formulation of an ethic of social justice was needlessly freighted with incompatibilities with historic Christianity and with internal contradictions that drew fire from right and left.

At several points evangelical and non-evangelical critics coalesced: namely, concerning the continuing discontinuity of the ideal and the historical on which Niebuhr insisted, and his complete dismissal of *agape* as a transforming social power. Evangelical and post-Niebuhrian critics forged their criticism out of quite different interests, to be sure. For evangelical Christianity, the standing Niebuhrian tension between the ideal and the historical did more than undermine simply the Genesis account of Adam in the divine image, whose fall plunged the whole race into sin; it undermined also the Gospel account of Jesus Christ as the incarnation of God in history, and drove Niebuhr to distinguish Christ as an ideal from the historical person, Jesus of Nazareth. Moreover, it ruled out not only the possibility of any final historical manifestation of the Kingdom of God, but also eroded the possibilities of Christian culture (even as a partial or limited achievement, in distinction from *a* Christian culture). And for evangelical Christianity also, the Niebuhrian dismissal of the social significance of individual regeneration and sanctification signaled an unjustifiable defection from the primary task of the church in the world, that of the spiritual evangelization of unregenerate humanity. Say what one will about exaggerated evangelical expectations from evangelism — and we shall later have some pointed things to say in this regard — Niebuhr's neglect of the indispensability of personal conversion not only underestimated the importance of love as a correlative of justice in a stable social order, but also required him to shift onesidedly to justice and to the state's coercive role a burden for social transformation that the state cannot really bear and ought not ideally to carry. Important as was Niebuhr's insight that group behavior has massive possibilities of self-deception, he was wrong in stressing that immorality is a product of social institutions, and is not rooted in individuals. In brief, the revolt against the Social Gospel doctrine of the gradual social incarnation of God might have been formulated in the context of orthodox Protestant ethics. But it was not, and the Niebuhrian alternative in its re-assertion of some aspects of the Christian tradition was as destructive of certain essential elements of the Biblical view as it was reconstructive of others.

The reaction against Niebuhr's formulation came, not surprisingly, from neo-Protestants who fastened on other neglected elements of the traditional view. Since, however, their newer theory itself was not forged essentially from the standpoint of evangelical ethics, but rather in terms of a double reaction — against Niebuhr's reaction from the Social Gospel — it incorporated several features highly dis-tasteful to the Niebuhrian approach, and others for which Niebuhrian ethics had unwittingly prepared the way.

3. *Revolutionary Ethics: Secular Theology*

From one point of view Niebuhrian ethics had deep built-in retards against a revolutionary ethic promotive of social-ism. For one thing, Niebuhr emphasized historical continu-ity above discontinuity. Moreover, his approach to social justice was analytical rather than revolutionary, and he shunned any expectation of literal eschatological fulfillment, contrary to those social critics who were otherwise influenced by the Marxian dialogue.

Yet Niebuhr himself viewed ethical conflict basically in terms of class conflict, and insisted that human groups are related more in terms of power than of moral concerns. He ranked government, or organized power, as higher in moral sanction and social necessity than the balance of power, which fact provided a theoretical basis for social-ism with its planned society. And his justification of violence ("its terror must have the tempo of a surgeon's skill and healing must follow quickly upon its wounds," *Moral Man and Immoral Society*, p. 220), although propounded in the context of support of justice against the assaults of injustice, could be readily misappropriated by those who were ready to abandon persuasion and judicial processes in their advocacy of guerilla violence as a means to social change.

The very criticisms of historical reason that Niebuhr invoked against socialism as a fixed and final social ideal could be turned against Niebuhr's own ethical stance by those who preferred to promote socialism. Niebuhr, it will be recalled, took issue with socialism on several grounds. Contrary to the socialist emphasis on man's continuity with nature, and its dismissal of all ultimate theological and moral categories for understanding man's capacity to react with and upon his environment, he stressed that history can be understood only in terms of the tension between man and God and between good and evil in human nature; this argument was essentially an evangelical criticism, except that Niebuhr instead employed ontological categories of his own making. He also stressed that man's reason is always partial and infected by self-interest, and that all value judgments are conditioned by one's social context, contrary to the socialist thesis that man's reason automatically unfolds an ethical order; power and life, Niebuhr argued, will always transcend reason, as opposed to the socialist confidence that historical power can be rationally and morally controlled. It was Niebuhr's rejection of final truth, in the interest of dialectical tension, and his relativizing of the entire content of man's knowledge, that supplied a major basis of evangelical critique: "If *no* truth is final, then it is not final either that the relation between time and eternity is dialectical or that *agape* defines the role of our free responsibilities" (Edward John Carnell, *The Theology of Reinhold Niebuhr*, 1951, p. 239). Seen from the perspective of historic Christianity, Niebuhr elevates man's corruption to a final principle of interpretation, and on this basis rejects the orthodox view of revelation (and sin); Biblical Christianity acknowledges revelation as definitively explanatory of sin, and does not regard sin as rendering revelation ambiguous. "The total depravity of man does not make revelation problematical

. . . . Revelation is the only authentic source for interpreting sin" (Theodore Minnema, *The Social Ethics of Reinhold Niebuhr*, n.d., p. 115).

Niebuhrian skepticism can be turned against any and all of Niebuhr's own finalities for the sake either of reviving consideration of the evangelical option or of projecting still another speculative alternative. Evangelicalism harbored deep dissatisfaction over Niebuhr's formulation; it decried his denials that Jesus of Nazareth is the historically perfect manifestation of *agape*, that *agape* as a rule of individual life has significant social consequences, and that man in any situation knows the will of God specifically. A recanvassing of the evangelical alternative would have revived interest, therefore, in the unique moral values associated with the life of Jesus of Nazareth in the context of God's supernaturally revealed will and commandments, and not in the mood of a secular theology. It would have done so, moreover, without sacrificing an important role for both love and justice in the social arena, by emphasizing the necessary function of government as an instrumentality of justice, warning of the defeat of pure love as a moral force in an unregenerate world, and calling immoral man to meet the Lord of life and history either in personal conversion or in eschatological doom.

But the turn from Niebuhr took another direction. The dialectical ethic had left in doubt the supernatural as a separate reality, and the historical arena remained as the one sure world of social responsibility. The next mood to captivate neo-Protestant social critics would be predicated not on sin as the final interpretive principle, nor on the gradual social incarnation of God, nor would it return to an authentically evangelical basis in supernatural revelation and the Word of God. It would be secular and pragmatic in orientation, rather than metaphysical. While it would scoff at evangelical enthusiasts who look to the miraculous conversion of individuals for the effective transformation of society, it would pin its own hope for universal justice on swift, revolutionary social change. Moreover, it would expedite this goal by direct pressures of the institutional church on government agencies for the adoption of specific politico-economic legislation to implement socialistically-oriented policies.

The 1966 Geneva Conference on Church and Society, sponsored by the World Council of Churches, attested the emergence of an influential post-Niebuhrian social ethic. In that conference ecumenical activists sought to commit institutional Christianity at the world level to a sanction of violence and revolution as a method of social change and to sustained socio-political pressures on governments for specific military and economic positions oriented to socialist perspectives.

What are the identifiable features of this more radical ethic? Its espousal of socialist ideals clearly shows its continuity with earlier ecumenical traditions in social ethics. The Social Gospel championed socialism in an uncritical way: it fleshed out the Kingdom of God, of which Jesus was the prophet, and in which divine immanence in history and rational human adjustment were conspiring toward its progressive realization in society. Niebuhr took a more critical stance — after an earlier Marxist stage — and stressed that to claim finality for socialism or any other historical form was idolatrous; he nevertheless remained an advocate of creeping socialism, although his latest commitments show a nod toward violence as a legitimate instrument for promoting social change.

Together with this inherited commitment to socialist ideals, ecumenical thought is increasingly committed to rapid social change. Radical religious secularists think that the time has come for galloping socialism, particularly in respect to the elimination of economic disparities. By historicizing the Christian doctrine of creation and eschatology, it seeks to provide a religious rationale of revolutionary change. Paul

Lehmann asserts that revolution is the cutting edge "of God's humanizing activity." To transform society it does not reinstate the traditional evangelical confidence in divine regeneration and its expectation of end-time judgment for inverting man and society; nor does it rely on immanent evolution and modernist enlightenment guided by Divine Reason. It tends to be skeptical of preaching and conversion as a social force and relies instead on direct political action.

The ethic of social revolution relies for its confrontation of social evils on mob pressure and government coercion — not enlightened by educational and judicial processes definitive of justice, but prodded by civil disobedience and violence supposedly ventured as acts of love. The earlier promotion of protest marches and picketing, then of campaigns of civil disobedience and economic boycotts, is now accelerated to contemplate physical disruption in which property rights are demeaned, violence is condoned, perpetuated and encouraged to redress wrong, and churches are used as sanctuaries for those who oppose the police-military arm of the state in ecclesiastically-approved conflicts. That such tactics are pro-revolutionary, and actually spawn the spirit of revolution among the discontented, gives the secular theologians of social revolution no qualms. They do no seem to sense that violence is self-defeating, that violence carries no guarantees of the actual results its sponsors seek or that they can control it once underway, or that violence in any event cannot provide the new society mankind so desperately needs.

Another feature of the ethic of revolution is its impatience with metaphysical concerns. It promotes an activistic rather than analytic approach to social concerns. So often does one hear that the secular mentality considers systematic treatises on the nature of the divine activity irrelevant that one easily gets the impression that the new social ethic prefers to reinforce rather than to challenge the secular outlook. What it encourages is presence and involvement and running dialogue at the dynamic frontiers of revolution, even if such identification simply raises questions rather than provides answers. Classic modernism moved from Hegelian metaphysics to the Social Gospel, and Niebuhrian ethics moved from an existential-dialectical view of man to the necessary role of collective power, but secular ethics leaps to action in metaphysical murkiness. This approach means the abandonment of a theistic rationale for social action; the appeal of *agape*, vaguely defined, is the last vestige of a Christian framework. Dialogue with Communists is now often pursued by an appeal to the "existential Marx" rather than to the "theoretical Marx." Recent scholars would contend that this distinction is unjustifiable; Marxists, however, insist that if such differentiation has a basis in fact, the authentic Marx is the later theoretical Marx and not an earlier Marx.

Today ecumenical social thinking challenges Marxism only *after Marxism comes to power.* This it does essentially on the ground of Niebuhr's criticism that when in power Marxism gets in the way of creative response to the problem of order and change. Harvey Cox points out that the contemporary theological understanding of revolution is based "on our understanding of human history, where God is at work, and of what he is doing in that history" *(The Church Amid Revolution,* 1967, p. 18). The Geneva Conference, significantly, voiced no condemnation of Communism. Ecumenical criticism in Geneva was reserved for anti-Communists. What "God" — and the W.C.C. as his instrument — apparently is doing in contemporary history is advancing Communism and opposing the forces that resist it. The ecumenical social revolutionaries urge that the church be "set free" as a revolutionary force so that it may be fully involved in contemporary revolutionary struggles. Their attempt to justify this revolutionary implementation of socialism in terms of eschatological fulfillment is a perverse misinterpretation of Biblical teaching. In the Bible, salvation is not the readjustment of man's social environment or the self-reformation of the world; the Bible considers the unregenerate world to be under the judgment of God even in the age of eschatological fulfillment.

The basic problem of modern society, as the secular revolutionaries see it, is that of economic inequality. The heart of their "gospel" is that Christ died for the redistribution of wealth and that these infinite material resources are now to be universally resurrected by secular ecumenism. This social ethics appeals to the self-interest of the masses: the poor are offered more of somebody else's hard-won possessions if only they will "trust the church" to implement a political means of self-aggrandizement, and of institutionalizing class warfare through punitive taxes that penalize those who earn more than others. The young are offered escape from military service. If these churchmen were also to offer sex fulfillment to everybody — by disregard for the inherited views of marriage — the pattern of self-gratification through secular religion would be complete, since it would condition man's relationships to the world of sex, economics and government. Since the religious-socialist state would now guarantee his new "liberty," he would forfeit freedom against the totalitarian state for "security" — in the name of Christ the Lord!

To Harvey Cox the secular revolutionary approach to social ethics is predicated actually on an evolutionary rather than on a creation-fall-redemption context for the understanding of history. By setting aside transcendent ontological categories, and particularly the objective truth of revealed religion, the notion can be expounded that all existing social structures are changeable. Current criticism gains support by its rejection of the idea that the social orders are sacred, and by its assertion that evangelical Christianity is committed to a defense of the *status quo*. It was classic modernism, interestingly enough — with its notion of exaggerated divine immanence — that viewed the social orders as sacred or directly continuous with the Kingdom of God. This has by no means been the view of evangelical Christian-

ity. No religious community is able wholly to divest itself
of dependence upon the culture of its day, and secular theologians today have less reason than anyone to exempt themselves. Protestant orthodoxy must nonetheless bring driving
criticism to bear upon the existing social orders by insisting
both on the social consequences of the fall and on the need
of supernatural divine redemption "far as the curse is found."
Yet orthodox Christianity would never say that the forms of
social existence are dispensable and replaceable or part of
an evolutionary process. What evangelical social ethics does
say is that the social context in relation to God's purpose in
creation is frustrated by the fall, but renewable by redemptive grace. Where social critics speak with Marx only of the
fluidity of a dynamic society, the social orders of marriage,
labor and economics, and civil government become merely
evolutionary developments of transitory significance. Evangelical ethics, however, views these structures in the creation-fall-redemption context and insists that they provide the
historical framework in which social justice ideally functions
in a fallen society.

While the social revolutionaries contend that they do not
return to the Social Gospel uncritically, they modify the con-
tention of the Niebuhrian dialectic that the ideal cannot be
achieved in history (Harvey Cox, On Not Leaving It to the
Snake, 1967, p. 138). They reassert the ideal of establishing
God's Kingdom on earth. They do not immediately expect
its full manifestation; its universal realization is thought to
require several pushes due to the intransigence of evil and
the perverseness of power. But they seek to establish certain
elements of the Kingdom. While they do not overtly identify
pacifism and socialism with the gospel, and their views tend
to be "more provisional" than were those of the Social Gospel era, their sympathies are clearly in this direction.

They view the church, moreover, more as an ally of secular agencies and viewpoints than as the vanguard of a distinctive message and movement. A secular theology must

necessarily secularize the church as well as all other New Testament entities. Whatever virtue the secular theology gains through its refusal to identify pacifism and socialism directly with the gospel is more than lost by its refusal to identify the gospel in Biblical terms and its diversion of the church from its apostolic mission. It is far more successful in altering the authentic content of Christianity and the proper task of the church than in changing the character of politics; instead of improving the political realms it is transforming institutional Christianity into a political mechanism. Although institutional ecumenism was originally a creation of the denominations, it is now reducing the denominations to dependency and redefining the doctrine of the church. Revision of the nature and task of the church in a secular way has become a live possibility because social revolutionaries now hold influential posts in the ecumenical bureaucracy and hold tenure on seminary faculties while they promote views opposed by the churches that gave rise to these structures. The secular revolutionaries are suspicious of all power structures except their own. But the assumption that social revolutionaries have political expertise because they are clergymen may in fact breed the most serious anti-clerical reaction in Protestant history.

III.

How then shall evangelical Christianity cope with neo-Protestant emphases in social affairs?

The temptation to stress evangelism only as "the Christian answer" and to withdraw from social confrontation is dangerous and one that Protestant orthodoxy had best avoid. For one thing, even secular social critics now champion an "evangelism" of sorts, reinterpreted to promote a change in social structures rather than the spiritual transformation of persons. But even if a secular non-evangelical "evangelism" were not now in vogue and with considerable ecumenical

sanction, evangelical Christianity would still make a serious
mistake to abandon the arena of social ethics. To do so would
guarantee the influential impact of only non-evangelical ideologies upon the intellectual community and in the public
arena.

The present time is, in fact, highly propitious for an evangelical witness in social affairs. The disturbing outbreaks in
otherwise placid segments of American society have reinforced a conviction that modern social theories do not elicit
the response of "good will" so essential to community stability and public well-being. The common virtues of revealed religion — such as neighbor-love, compassion, pa-
tience, industry, faithfulness — are precisely what seem to
have declined during the heyday of non-evangelical social
theories; one of their hallmarks, in point of fact, is an aver-
sion to traditional ethical emphases. Moreover, the vast confusion in ecumenical circles today — the lack of a unifying
theology, of an agreed philosophy of evangelism, of a common definition of the gospel — now coincides with widening
disparity over the nature and philosophy of ecumenical social involvement. This turn of affairs in the world and in the
institutional church confers upon evangelical Christians new
and unprecedented opportunities to speak at the important
frontiers of contemporary decision — in regard to birth control and all the problems of sex life and the family; in regard
to labor, technology, wealth and poverty, work and leisure,
and other critical concerns in economics; in regard to government, war and peace, and all the problems of justice in
today's world. Opportunity for a social witness to the message of revealed religion for modern man is at high tide, and
if evangelical Christianity hopes to confront the present generation with a sure sense of the undeniable relevance of traditional Christianity for the last third of the twentieth century, then the evangelical vanguard must not forego this
chance nor evade this duty.

The first order of business in presenting an evangelical

social ethic is to expose the false assumptions that control the contemporary alternative. Sometimes these unconscious assumptions are uncritically assumed to constitute the only defensible rationale for thought and action, and are therefore taken wholly for granted. Merely to challenge the subordinate theses that flow from these controlling concepts is like trying to extinguish a raging forest fire by watering down the branches of a few isolated trees. Worse yet, these modern prejudices so dominate the contemporary spirit that it seems to many inconceivable that anything else should have motivated the first Christians. It becomes all the more important, therefore, to begin with what is surely known about the earliest followers and ambassadors of Jesus Christ. We need to ask not whether their outlook on Christianity and the world accords with ours, but whether the contemporary view can really be identified with theirs.

If we examine the main tenets controlling the outlook of New Testament Christians in relation to the world around them, we find this much to be certain:

(1) They expected the climax of human felicity not in this earthly existence, but in a blessed afterlife. It never occurred to them to immanentize the eschatological, that is, to look for the zenith of happiness this side of physical death and resurrection. To be "with Christ," wrote the apostle Paul, is not simply "better," but "far better" (Phil. 1:23). Again, "if Christ be not risen, then is your faith vain" (I Cor. 15:14). Loss of the supernatural world in which righteousness reigns and redeemed sinners share endless glory would have meant for them that the Christian religion is a tragic illusion. The early Christians could never have inverted Christ's teaching to read: "Blessed are ye, though you lose your soul, if you gain the whole world."

(2) They connected fullness of life and enduring meaning with a personal relation to Christ and his regenerate church. Nowhere did they encourage those outside of Christ and of the fellowship of the redeemed to think that they could find

abundant life and a permanently rewarding existence apart
from new life in Christ and outside the Christian community.
Throughout the New Testament the distinction between
church and world is never obscured; the world is exposed to
God's wrath, and its destiny is doom; the church is a haven
of redemption, and its destiny is glory.

(3) Least of all did the early Christians encourage the notion that fallen man's permanent felicity and ideal existence
can be achieved through the reorganization of his material
environment — whether by socio-economic changes or by
scientific techniques and comforts. Although justice in the
political order was God's will indeed, and injustice a dam-
nable thing, nowhere did the early Christians suggest that
the permanent expectation solely of justice was a hopeful
condition for sinful man. The church's message was not
simply that God wills justice for and by all, but that God in
mercy offers justification to sinners otherwise exposed to divine condemnation. New Testament Christianity always finds
the locus of human hope not in *gnosis* — or trust in man's
justice or ingenuity — but in *grace* as a divine provision.

(4) The early Church knew itself to be ideally a regenerate
and renewed remnant of humanity entrusted with a divinely-
given mission that centers in addressing individuals with the
redemptive good news. The New Testament nowhere declares the current view that the church's role in society takes
precedence over her inner life — of worship, study, and holiness — and that only after altering the social structures can
she discover how to be renewed.

(5) The early church faced the world of its day by bold
proclamation of the standards by which God will judge men
and nations, of the gospel of Christ's redemptive rescue,
and by exemplary obedience to the will of God, including
devotion to justice in the public realm to the limit of their
competence. Nowhere does the New Testament provide the
institutional church any authority, jurisdiction, or mandate
to wield direct pressure upon government and public agen-

cies for commitment to specific ecclesiastically-approved policies and programs. The church had no revelational solutions to secular specifics; nonetheless it encouraged all Christians to fulfill their duties as citizens of two worlds in devout obedience to the commandments of God.

(6) While the New Testament indicates that disobedience may at times be a spiritual duty, it does not encourage a revolutionary attitude toward the state. Oscar Cullmann notes that the entire New Testament is characterized by Jesus' attitude that although the state is not a final divine institution, it does have a legitimate role; every attempt to overthrow it is therefore renounced (*The State in the New Testament*, 1956, pp. 18 f.). The New Testament instances in which Christians disobeyed rulers involve refusal to yield to attempts to suppress the proclamation of the gospel. Fulfillment of the Great Commission was explicitly commanded, and in this mission the followers of Christ were constrained to obey God rather than men. In Romans 13:8-10 the apostle Paul instructs the early Christians that they will best avoid punishment at the hands of pagan rulers by keeping the social commandments of the Decalogue. The New Testament sets absolutely no precedent for the church's advocacy of mob pressures and guerilla violence as ways of implementing socio-economic changes; the early Christians relied on proclamation, persuasion, and example.

(7) The New Testament views the roots of the social orders of marriage and the family, of labor and economics, and of civil government to be in the will of God and not as contingent evolutionary emergents in society that have temporary significance and are subject to revision and displacement as historical forms. To God's revealed will the New Testament ascribes the ideals of permanent monogamous marriage, of "work and eat" and "work and rest" as the framework of man's earthly vocation, and of the state as a coercive force to promote order and preserve justice in a fallen society.

In summary, an authentic Christian social ethic begins with the surety of the self-revealing God as creator, redeemer and judge of all, and of the soul as a sensorium of the eternal supernatural world — in contrast to merely world-affirming secular ethics which shrivels the realm of reality. It associates man's ideal existence above all else with conformity to the likeness of Jesus Christ, a conformity that finds its supreme fulfillment in the eschatological future, contrasted with the Social Gospel (which immanentizes Christ and the Kingdom), with secular ethics (which historicizes everything), and with Niebuhrian ethics (which distinguishes Jesus of Nazareth from the Christ). An authentic Christian social ethic, moreover, finds in "the redemption that is in Christ Jesus" alone, and in personal inclusion in the regenerate body He heads, the only sure source of an abundant and permanently meaningful existence, in contrast to Niebuhrian ethics (which silences the demand for universal conversion) and secular ethics (which shrouds the Biblical contrast of church and world). Its confidence is in divine grace as a human change-agent, and not in human *gnosis* as an environmental transformant. An authentic evangelical ethic, moreover, understands the church as a redeemed remnant of mankind whose calling as the people of God is first and foremost the obedient worship of the Crucified and Risen Lord, the One who by the Spirit indwells and renews his followers. In contrast, activists stress that the church *is* mission, and assign social involvement precedence over the inner life of the church. The early church faced the world, rulers included, in and through the proclamation of God's revealed commandments and the gospel of grace; in contrast, ecumenical social ethics concentrates on specific instructions to governments in day-to-day politico-economic decisions. The early church viewed its role in relation to civil government in terms of prayerful accord and loyalty that were limited only by the superior claim of the Ruler of the universe whose revealed purpose for both church and state had been made known; in contrast, the current tendency is to mobilize church opinion for civil disobedience and mob pressures even where avenues of persuasion have not been exhausted. The early church approached the basic orders of social life as created and fallen, and in need of redemptive renewal; the modern ecclesiastical assault, on the other hand, approaches society on the basis of a fluid society subject to evolutionary change.

An inversion of the apostolic perspectives will clarify the ideological hinterland of what now often passes for Christian social ethics: the changing temporal-historical world becomes the one sure reality within which the church is called to speak and act; in this socio-historical context is to be found the ultimate climax and destiny of human existence; the abundant life and enduring personal meaning and happiness depend upon environmental reconstruction to eliminate economic disparity, physical disease and social insecurity; social scientists and politicians are the potent midwives of the Kingdom of God on earth; the institutional church has the political role of articulating specific legislative positions and military decisions, of instructing public officials that moral fulfillment requires their approval of these particular views, and implementing these views as official commitments through direct political pressures; the modern church is called, moreover, to identify itself with the revolutionary forces in society at the frontiers of social change; and the Christian approach to the social orders must be radical-eschatological.

When such inverted guidelines of social ethics are brought into the open — either as deliberatively held positions, or as unconscious assumptions, or as conditioning influences in the absence of any alternative — two facts are patently clear.

One is that man's environment, the real world as it truly is, is here falsified almost wholly beyond Biblical cognizability. While the Scriptural vocabulary is often retained — and indeed the familiar terms creation, fall, redemption, eschatology, Christ, church, are worked and overworked into the current ecclesiastical literature — these leading motifs of revealed religion are emptied of traditional connotations and given a novel allegorical or symbolical turn. Creation and eschatology are historicized; the fall is not what Paul and the early Christians believed, nor is redemption; and the Christ is something other than Jesus of Nazareth, the incarnate Logos. Nobody should then be surprised that the Church is no longer assuredly the Church in its New Testament self-understanding. For once the awesome reality of God is lost as the sovereign, independent Creator of a contingent universe, and man is no longer bound to intelligible divine revelation and to the will of God expressed in articulate commandments, then the ensuing picture of the human predicament and of the world of reality is a caricature. Those who think of man's environment only in terms of a one-layer world of reality are self-deceived, and their untruth about God leads to the distortion of much else. One must believe in magic, in the power of clever words to eclipse the supernatural world from modern significance, to think that the new secular mood in religious social ethics provides an authentic ideological framework for Christian social ethics.

The second consideration is this, that the universe of discourse in Christian social ethics is now highly weighted with concerns emphasized by the Communist view of man and the universe. It is no accident that the time is considered especially propitious for Christian-Communist dialogue. The surviving theological mood in ecumenical circles tapers the doctrine of creation to the processes of "historicized" nature, and that of eschatology to Christ's "ever-coming present triumph over the powers." All of this is compatible with a constant appeal to "what God is doing in the world" in order to promote *ad hoc* positions, and these predominantly socialist in stance. The secular theologians, moreover, have abandoned belief in a transcendent, personal God who has acted supernaturally in history and revealed himself objectively in his incarnate Son and in sacred Scripture; they now welcome Marx's view of the dialectical nature of human history and identify themselves with Marx's plea that secular man grasp the historical initiative in order to master the modern world. Harvey Cox deplores "the strident anti-communism of the churches," Paul Lehmann credits Marx with exposing the supposedly "great error" of the Christian view of God's immutability in relation to man and history, and Leslie Dewart praises "the common humanistic concern of both Christianity and Marxism." The key word in ecclesiastical engagement at political frontiers today is *confrontation,* a term that has deteriorated from its transcendent, supernatural orientation in the theology of recent decades. Cox claims that Christians must learn from the Marxists that all human thought, including theological thought (except, of course, this interpretive secular conceptuality of revelational *gnosis!*), is shaped by a concrete historical situation. The ironical turn is that while in the name of dynamic creativity the ecumenical church has virtually conformed the rationale and content of ecumenical social ethics to socialism, in the name of Jesus Christ it is now spawning a culture-Christianity that is predicated on modern secularism. That Communism is benevolent, and that Christians should cooperate in advancing its social objectives, as a providential manifestation of the Kingdom of God, is an emphasis increasingly registered in ecumenical circles; capitalism is somehow held to be discontinuous with the will of God, and communism continuous with it; capitalism is said to require divine judgment, and to be defensible only in terms of uncritical commitment to the *status quo,* while the social goals of Communism are depicted as an aspect of spiritual redemption required by dynamic historical progress.

In this dual development — the forsaking of the supernatural and the acceptance of an essentially Marxist view of history — the loss of a sure word of God and of the fixed will of God is an inevitable result. If God is abandoned as the sovereign controller of the historical process who encounters man in every historical situation, and instead — if still tolerated — has a "history" of his own, and is caught in temporal relativities and corrupted by cultural configurations, then no possibility remains for transcendent divine commandments and an unchanging right and duty. In this event it is only pious double-talk to speak of God achieving a redemptive purpose in the concrete realities of history. But what this development signifies is not the final truth and ultimate triumph of Communism, but the remarkable prevision of revealed religion. For the apostle Paul speaks of a generation so perverse that it neither glorifies God nor is thankful — of men who no longer say *yes* to God because, it may be, they think they have trapped him in nature and history, and have him at their own mercy, or perchance because they have no religious concern other than to be forever theologically a la mode. Such a generation God gives up to the self-deception of human pride, and simply reminds of final judgment to come.

The definition of the social problem therefore gains a strikingly diverse formulation from the perspectives of evangelical and of secular theology. On the newer view, we are told that a secular future is now overtaking the whole earth, due to technological changes, population growth and industrialization. On the traditional view, alienation from God is man's natural fallen condition, and unless his heart is changed every social development becomes a new occasion for expressing his rebellion; the emergence of secular theology confirms rather than discredits the fact. On the newer view, the emergence of secularization requires a new secular theology — if Christianity is to retain cultural relevance. On the traditional view, contemporary disobedience requires the New Testament revelation; the non-supernatural restatements of the Gospel are really culture-bound rationalizations. Evangelical Christianity insists that the long run of history discloses man's own inability to eliminate historical evil. But it emphasizes that there is an actual redemptive working of God in history, and that God achieves his redemptive purpose in part in the concrete historical situation.

The Theology 3
of Evangelism

Two milleniums ago no church as yet existed in the New Testament sense. The community of faith that survived Old Testament times was neither buoyant with joy nor bright with hope. Awaiting the salvation of Israel were devout figures like Simeon for whom the prophetic promises were still alive, and through Zachariah and Elizabeth and Joseph and Mary the economy of redemption moved suddenly toward fulfillment. John the Baptist's call to repentance and renewal identified Jesus of Nazareth as the promised Redeemer. The three years of Jesus' public ministry have stimulated more comment and literature across nineteen centuries than any other comparable segment of human history.

Before Jesus' crucifixion many Jews had come to believe that he was indeed the Messiah of Old Testament prophecy. But Jesus' death routed those messianic hopes, and even his most trusted disciples were scattered and dismayed. Just how deeply disillusioned they must have been can only be measured by remembering that during the three years they had companied with the Nazarene, his life, teaching and works had elicited their confession that he was truly the promised Christ. For his open-ended calling and mission they had gladly forsaken family, friends and vocation.

Then came Jesus' death on the cross and with it the death

of every last vestige of messianic expectation. "We had hoped," they sighed, "that he would be the one who was going to redeem Israel" (Luke 24:21). The past perfect tense "we had hoped" emptied the present of every last remnant of faith and mirrors the dismal mood of Jesus' followers, At this point, there was neither a church in the New Testament sense, nor was there an evangel in the New Testament sense; there was no good news. In fact, the worst news possible had leadened the hearts of Jesus' committed followers: he had been crucified and buried.

Frederic W. Farrar, that devout Anglican scholar of an earlier day, described the mood of that crucifixion weekend like this: "At the moment when Christ died, nothing would have seemed more abjectly weak, more pitifully hopeless, more absolutely doomed to scorn and extinction, and despair, than the Church which he had founded. It numbered but a handful of weak followers, of which the boldest had denied his Lord with blasphemy, and the most devoted had forsaken him and fled. They were poor, they were ignorant, they were hopeless. They could not claim a single synagogue or a single sword. . . . So feeble were they and insignificant, that it would have looked like foolish partiality to prophesy for them the limited existence of a Galilean sect" (Frederic W. Farrar, *The Life of Christ*, London: Cassell & Company, Limited, 1887, pp. 453 f.).

Against this background let us consider crucial features that mark the momentous theology and the theological momentum of the Early Church.

1. The bodily resurrection of Jesus Christ is the only convincing explanation for the existence of the Christian church as an evangelistic movement in the world. It alone can explain the fact that Jesus' death changed into an indispensable item of good news, and became the first proposition that Christianity affirms as the world's best and only durable good news. "How was it," asks Farrar, "that these dull and ignorant men, with their cross of wood, tri-

umphed over the deadly fascination of sensual mythologies, conquered kings and their armies, and overcame the world? . . . There is one, and one only *possible* answer — the resurrection from the dead. All this vast revolution was due to the power of Christ's resurrection" (*ibid.*, p. 454). From the very first Christians were impelled to declare not simply that the one living God demands goodness in the lives of his worshipers, integral as that affirmation was to their faith. They felt impelled to assert also that Jesus Christ had risen from the dead in the immediate past, and that in this Risen One God had climaxed his work of salvation.

Without this resurrection of Jesus of Nazareth neither the Christian church nor the New Testament would have come into being. "Christ died and is risen according to the Scriptures" — around this fixed axis revolve the life of the early Christians and the letters of the apostles. Time and again the apostolic message, whether addressed to Jew or Gentile, returns to the convinced fact of the bodily resurrection of the Crucified Jesus; this event headlines the good news. We read that the Sanhedrin acknowledged Jesus' tomb to be empty (Matt. 28:12 f.). The apostles, moreover, were chosen from those who conversed with Jesus in his resurrection appearances and who earlier had known him intimately during the days of his flesh (Acts 1:21). Now their ministry consisted first and foremost of testifying to the fact that they knew this crucified Jesus to be personally alive after his death.

Even Saul of Tarsus, when personally convinced of Jesus' resurrection, abandoned his role as the Sanhedrin's official archpersecutor of the first Christians to become, instead, Christianity's greatest apostle to the Gentiles. In writing to the Corinthians he identifies what he now delivers to them to be of priority importance, namely, that "Christ died for our sins according to the Scriptures, and was buried, and rose again the third day according to the Scriptures, and was seen . . ." (I Cor. 15:3 f.). This message he himself had received as the core of primitive Christian preaching.

It was the resurrection, and that alone which inverted Jesus' crucifixion into good news and into a necessary part of the total good news; the resurrection showed Jesus' death to be not an ignominious catastrophe but rather a divine provision. "God so loved the world," writes the apostle John in words to become as immortal as any in the annals of history, "that he gave his only Son, that whosoever believeth in him shall not perish but have everlasting life" (John 3:16). The divine prerogatives claimed for Jesus of Nazareth by the early Christians are asserted not in spite of, but because of his suffering and shame and death. "Jesus our Lord," writes Paul, "was delivered for our offenses, and was raised again for our justification" (Romans 4:24 f.). Scripturally expounded, that death and resurrection are the God-constituted ground of the redemption of doomed sinners; they are the heart of the Christian evangel for the world. The death of Jesus of Nazareth was indispensable, but without his bodily resurrection the Christian church would have been still-born.

2. The early Christians knew the crucified Jesus not only as risen, however; they knew him now also as the Ascended and Exalted Lord personally and manifestly present in their midst. The reality of the resurrection had stirred a Copernican-like revolution in their understanding of Jesus' death; no less remarkable now was the reorientation of their lives to Jesus after the spirit rather than after the flesh. Those who had shared Jesus' earthly three-year companionship treasured incomparable privileges and unforgettable experiences of his example and teaching of trust, prayer, love, self-denial and humility. Yet in the weeks after his burial they suddenly demote these memories. Something cataclysmic transforms their nostalgic longings and replaces them with current new relationships and confident expectations of a future that they recognize as superior. Their feelings of homesickness are inverted: "We have a sample of our

inheritance" (Eph. 1:14), they testify. The reunion to which
they now aspire looks to the Ascended Christ, to the one who
through death and resurrection had already preceded them
into the eternal realm.

What stupendous happening accounts for this remarkable
spiritual inversion? The answer, in a word, is Pentecost.
At Pentecost the Risen Jesus met them in the promised
gift of the Holy Spirit, and transformed them into new
men, new women — indeed, into a new fellowship. They
were now permanently indwelt and personally enlivened by
the Holy Spirit in whom their invisible Lord was himself
present and active in their lives. Jesus had said and it
had now come to pass: "I will pray the Father, and he shall
give you another Comforter, that he may abide with you
for ever. . . . I will not leave you orphans: I will come to
you. . . . At that day ye shall know that I am in my
Father, and ye in me, and I in you" (John 14:16 ff.).

The modern church is often thought of as a building
where a specialist lectures once or twice a week to com-
muting parishioners who in turn keep the place and program in good repair by dropping a dollar — more or less —
into the offering plate. While the early Christians made
their own and many mistakes, they never made this one, or
they would have had to disown their very identity. They
knew and were convinced that the church of Jesus Christ is a
fellowship of the twice-born, or of "born of God" persons (John 1:13). Sad to say, modern churches are often
comprised of people unsure whether or not they are really
Christians. The early Christians knew that active faith in
the Crucified and Risen Redeemer requires putting one's
body on the line.

These primitive believers knew, moreover, that the as-
sembled church is not merely a horizontal fellowship of
humans, important as that is. However few in number,
they knew that they gathered not only with each other
but also and especially with the Risen and Exalted Lord in

their midst (Matt. 18:20). The church was, in fact, a spec-
tacle even to the angels; it was a showcase of and into the
invisible world, the locus of God's special activity in history, a heavenly outpost for the Kingdom of God in human
society. Built on the confession that Jesus is "the Christ,
the Son of the living God" (Matt. 16:16), this Body was
the feet and hands and lips of its Risen Head.

In day to day living the early Christians displayed virtues
that could only stagger the pagan mind and heart — new
powers of love, joy, kindness and peace (Gal. 5:22), virtues
that created advance interest for their witness and in
themselves as men newly alive from the grip of sin and
fear of death. Christ died, they said, not only that man's
sin would be covered by the Redeemer's righteousness, but
also that men might have a motivating trust that conquers
wrong. The early Christians showed, moreover, that they
valued this world's goods far less than the gifts of God.
Meeting from house to house for fellowship meals, and for
praise and prayer, many pooled material resources to meet
the needs of their members.

"They said that a new spirit was in them and among
them," writes R. W. Moore, "that as surely as Jesus of Nazareth had lived among them (as they could bear witness)
doing strange and wonderful things and speaking 'as never
yet man spake,' so surely and effectively his spirit was still
at work in their midst" *(The Furtherance of the Gospel,*
Toronto: Oxford University Press, 1950, p. 6). This new spirit
was, of course, the Holy Spirit, whom the apostle Paul had
early assayed as "not for nothing . . . called the Holy Spirit"
(I Thess. 4:8). They aspired to be conformed to Jesus Christ
"the same yesterday, today, and forever" (Heb. 13:8), rather
than to the mobile fashions of this world and to the social
prejudices of their day; they were indeed being remade
spiritually in the image of Christ. Knowing that the Ascended
Jesus had already carried human nature into the eternal
order "whither our forerunner is for us entered," as the

writer of Hebrews 6:20 puts it, they cherished that coming day when they would live totally free of sin and in the presence of Christ. "Your real life is Christ," Paul wrote them, "and when he appears, then you too will appear with him and share his glory" (Col. 3:4). The fact and experience of Pentecost marked them off forever from those unempowered days when "the Holy Spirit was not yet given" (John 7:39). The daily privilege of appropriating the Holy Spirit's filling deepened their delight in spiritual surrender; they knew that life unfilled by the Spirit of God dishonors and is below the dignity of Christian discipleship. The resurrection of Jesus Christ had originally vanquished their fear of death; now abundant life in the Spirit advertised for all the world to see that what men outside salvation called life was little more than a living death.

3. The church's task in the world was defined by the Risen Lord, to whom the church owes her origin, destiny and mission. From the very beginning the church perceived her foundation and destiny to be above and beyond the world in which she labors, recognizing in the Lord's advent and resurrection the dawning already now of the last days (Heb. 1:3). The climax of human bliss, those first Christians knew, turns on Christ's second advent and his vindication of righteousness and final judgment of evil; no dream of this worldly utopia could crowd out the central importance of their personal relationship to Jesus Christ.

The church's earthly vocation was formulated by the Lord of the church. At one stage Jesus commanded: "Go not into the way of the Gentiles" (Matt. 10:5). But, thank God, after his resurrection and before his ascension he reversed that charge: "Ye shall receive power, the Holy Ghost coming upon you," he said, "and ye shall be witnesses unto me in Jerusalem, and in all Judea and Samaria, and unto the uttermost part of the earth" (Acts 1:8). What more dramatic change of course can be imagined than the redirection of revealed redemptive religion from the Hebrew

to the Gentile world? What was first entrusted to the Jews
was now, by Jewish disciples of Jesus of Nazareth, aggressively carried to "the Jew first, but the Greek also" (Rom.
1:16), in the portentous awareness that "partial blindness
has come upon Israel . . . until the Gentiles have been
admitted in full strength" (Rom. 11:25, New English Bible).

The Great Commission was given by the Risen Lord
himself (Matt. 28:19 f.), a fact that sets the Magna Charta
of Christianity above that of any and all other movements
in world history. Under this aegis the apostle Paul went
even to Athens, that haven of the classic Greek philosophers,
not to remind them of Plato's vision of justice in the *Republic,*
but to proclaim "Jesus and the resurrection" (Acts 17:18).
What obedient fulfillment of the Great Commission entails
is seen in the preaching of the apostles as recorded in Acts.
Technically speaking, everything that Scripture teaches is
kerygma or prophetic-apostolic witness; more narrowly, the
kerygma is the good news that because of the incarnation,
atonement and resurrection of the Logos, and the consequent
exaltation of Jesus as Lord, we may have forgiveness of sins
and new spiritual life.

The early Christians knew that the eternal Logos had
become flesh and had therefore become what he was not
(John 1:14), in order that sinners might become what they
are not, namely, the moral and spiritual sons of God (John
1:12). They knew, moreover, that by their special task in
the world they had been integrated into the redemptive
covenant of the Godhead; as the Son had stepped into
history from the outside, so now he had dispatched them
into the remaining history of the world with a trans-histori-
cal, trans-cultural message. Not until the fact that he had
been divinely *sent,* and its implications for total obedience
in life and word even unto death had become clear, did
Jesus enunciate the words "as the Father hath sent me
into the world, so send I you" (John 17:18).

Jesus deliberately oriented the Jewish controversy concerning his messianic mission to the unitary purpose and work and nature of the Father and the Son. The choice to be made is not between either the Father or the Son, but rather between both Father and Son or neither Father nor Son (John 5:17-23). Jesus' pointed reminder, "He that honoreth not the Son honoreth not the Father that sent him" (John 5:23) introduces a crescendo of statements that reiterate and reinforce Jesus' self-identification as the divinely sent one (cf. John 5:24, 30, 37, 38). In the healing of the man blind from birth, who is told "Go, wash in the pool of Siloam which" (as the Scripture informs us) "is by interpretation, Sent" (John 9:7) the thrust reaches its dramatic climax. The Sending Father and the Sent Son summarize the God of promise and fulfillment. The Great Commission integrates the disciples into God's redemptive covenant on the presupposition of Christ's accomplished atonement.

For the early Christians the Divine Trinity was not simply a theological doctrine but a practical and devotional reality: they had been dispatched into the world by the Son, whom the Father had sent, and the Father and the Son had poured out the Spirit upon them for their mission, and now indwelt them by that Spirit (John 14:23). The apostles are "sent-forth ones" whose evangelistic and missionary mission preserves the ongoing relay of the good news to mankind. "We are ambassadors on behalf of Christ, as though God were entreating by us: we beseech you on behalf of Christ, be ye reconciled to God" (II Cor. 5:20).

The believing church cannot guarantee that men will respond affirmatively. Yet her task is to see that men do not turn to pseudo-lords because of the lack of a compelling witness to the Crucified and Risen Son of God. To the early Christians it was now just as unthinkable that they should not witness to the world as that the God of redemptive mercy should not send his Son. "If God had not sent his Son . . . if we do not go" were part and parcel of one and the same strategic relationship to the plight of the world. The early Christians witnessed to Christ everywhere, refusing to allow philosophers to intimidate them or rulers to suppress the gospel. Their one fear was the fear of failure in fulfilling their mandate: "It is necessary to obey God rather than men" (Acts 5:29), they said. Their Risen Lord's "Go!" was the thrust that sent them to the ends of the earth.

They drew no lines of culture or race in winning men to Christ and to the church. They knew that the Logos who had assumed human flesh had in that same body conquered sin and death for all mankind. Those who were Gentiles knew that God's grace alone had included them no less than Jews in the family of redemption; as they put it, whether it was the Ethiopian eunuch, Saul of Tarsus, Cornelius of Caesarea, Timothy of Lystra, Dionysius and Damaris of Athens, or the saints in Caesar's household — "*the Lord added* to them day by day those that were being saved" (Acts 2:47). No one was more or less worthy than another of fellowship in the church and of a place in paradise; all men, and themselves most of all, these early Christians knew to be unworthy of God's grace. They were humbled and awed that God should rescue sinful men from "every tribe, and tongue, and people and nation" (Rev. 9:5). The early church was interested, moreover, in men and women individually as candidates for rehumanization for a divine destiny in this life and in the life to come, irrespective of racial or cultural or national striations. Few emphases obtrude more clearly in the New Testament than the awareness that the Exalted Lord himself directs and deploys his church for this global task. "*He gave* some to be apostles; and some, prophets; and some, evangelists; and some, pastors and teachers; for the perfecting of the saints, unto the work of ministering, unto the building up of the body of Christ . . ." (Eph. 4:11 f., American Standard Edition). To recall men to their created dignity, to rescue them from sin's hell and death, to renew them in salvation's grace and power, to awaken their sense of eternal destiny, and to renew them in the image of God, the church gave herself in glad obedience to the Great Commission of her Risen Head, and regarded fulfillment of this evangelistic mandate as her Number One task in the world.

4. The early Christians were commissioned to work in this present world. However keen were their expectations for the world to come, they knew that God had sent his Son into *this* world, that in *this* world they were to carry good news in his name and that in *this* world (even if they were not of it) they had a legitimate and necessary citizenship. Instead of forsaking this fallen world they were to bring to it the good news of redemption and of a better hope.

The implications of such dual citizenship were not at first nor at once wholly evident or clear. This seeming lack is often explained by the early Christians' expectation of an imminent if not immediate end of the world-order and inauguration of the eschatological end-time. This explanation may indeed fit small groups like the Thessalonians whom Paul instructed to return to their work and to whom he stressed that the end-time would not precede but would follow certain significant historical developments not yet realized. Many first-generation Christians had had personal contact with the earthly ministry of Jesus of Nazareth, hundreds had seen him alive again after his crucifixion and all of them shared the event of Pentecost as well as the dramatic news of the conversion of Saul of Tarsus and his special mission to the Gentiles. Surely the Christian community eagerly anticipated the climax toward which all these remarkable events are even yet moving. The resurrection of the crucified Jesus was in fact not only a sample of end-time history, but in some sense it already ushered in the last days.

Yet the end-time expectations of these believers were hedged about by certain very evident factors. The Risen Lord who would someday return was now already related to his followers in a distinctive interim way. Pentecost brought the indwelling Christ into the lives of believers as a permanent reality. The missionary mandate, moreover, demanded their carrying the gospel to the ends of the earth. Paul's letter to the Corinthians expounds God's final eschatological goals in view of Christ's resurrection, but his letter to the Romans expounds God's present purpose in civil government, to which Christian subjection is exhorted not simply as a matter of expedience but also of conscience.

Christian commitment in this world had for its governing presupposition the lordship of Christ as the ruler of nature, the sovereign of the nations and the decisive center of history. The negative consequences of these premises became apparent more readily and swiftly than positive implications. That Christ is the divine agent in the creation and the redemption of the cosmos frees nature of a presumed and presumptive enslavement to false gods. "For in him were all things created, in the heavens and upon the earth, things visible and invisible, whether thrones or dominions or principalities or powers; all things have been created through him and unto him; and he is before all things, and in him all things consist" (Col. 1:16 f.). Nature is thus freed in principle from the speculative pretenses of polytheism and gnosticism. So, too, Christ as King of kings and Lord of lords undercuts not only pagan worship of earthly rulers as epiphanies of the Divine, but also presumptive claims of the so-called divine right of kings. The Lordship of Christ, although asserted in the context of his yet future return, even now frees nature from the necessary service of pseudo-lords to serve instead the one and true Lord of lords. The way is thus first prepared for the coming in due time of natural science — in order that man may rule and use the cosmos under God in constructive ways. The way is prepared also for the gradual rise of political science whereby man may shape and use civil government under God in constructive ways. But miscarriage of that new freedom has brought Western man to the modern civilizational crisis.

Instead of investing his new freedom in respect to nature
and history under God and for the will of God, he now seeks
rather to exploit nature and history for selfish ends, in
marked detachment from the true Lord of the cosmos and
of the nations, and on the assumption of the irrelevance
of God.

It is in this context that the church must understand the
social dimension of her witness. The evangel that man is
divinely called to implement is not, to be sure, some socio-
political program or political ideology. But the good news
of a work of God's doing, the benefits of which fallen man
is invited to share, includes the prospect of new life and
of a new heavens and a new earth wherein dwelleth righteousness. The new society of the family of the redeemed is
called to mirror in microcosm. To the whole community of
mankind the church is called to proclaim the whole counsel
of God and to seek by persuasion to evoke universal com-
mittal to his commands. Never is the church more effective
in doing so than when she provides a living example in
her own ranks of what new life in Christ implies, and never
is she more impotent than when she imposes new standards
on the world that she herself neglects. A social ethic is not
some kind of bureaucratic imposition by the church upon
the world, but a mirroring to the world of the joys and
benefits of serving the living God.

Whether Christian or not, all men and all nations as well,
are accountable for social righteousness; God has willed
civil government in this fallen world to preserve justice and
to promote order. The church of Christ, we must remember,
is a minority movement whose historical impact is limited
not only by the willful resistance of the world as such but
also by the retarding effect of sin even in her own ranks.
But the Christian, because he knows the revealed commands
of God, can and should and must contribute energetically
to the debate over social justice. The Christian community

as a whole, moreover, has its own special opportunity to appropriate and demonstrate it.

Unless God's law and commands are represented with Biblical fidelity, the warning of the sharp edge of God's wrath, of the doom of entire nations to extinction in history, of the fearful truth of God's final judgment, and of the impending condemnation of unrepentant mankind will go unheeded. The early Christians knew that the amazing mercy of God's justification of sinners through Christ's substitutionary merit goes hand in hand with the awesome terror of God's justice. The Apostle of Love who wrote John 3:16 wrote also John 3:18, naming as already condemned those who do not believe on the name of the Son of God. Modern portraits of Jesus as an exponent only of God's love present but a partial picture; the gospels contain also the so-called severe sayings of Jesus which are distributed in almost equal proportion throughout all the supposed literary sources of the gospel writings. Rejection of the sent Son of God bears awesome penalties not only in the life to come but in this present life also.

Christians may and must work with non-Christians anywhere and everywhere in mutual quest and pursuit of social justice. The early Christians who lived in a context where the Roman jurists, and before them the Greek sages, spoke and wrote extensively of justice in society had no desire to demean such concern. Long before the great Greek philosophers had demanded social righteousness the Old Testament prophets had done so, and in greater depth. This prophetic vision of a messianic era of global goodness and cosmic peace the New Testament believers retained and promulgated. They knew, too, the obligation of government, however pagan, to preserve equality before the law; on that premise Paul had appealed to Caesar when fellow Jews frustrated a fair judicial hearing by Palestinian magistrates. Not all early Christians may have known the social vision of Plato's *Republic* despite which ancient Greece

crumbled; their children's children, however, lived to see
Rome smolder in ruins despite the Justinian *Code*. The
problem of society — though all the classic philosophers
condoned infanticide, temple prostitution, slavery and much
else — was not simply that pagan standards were lower than
God's commandments. The root problem was really that
mankind lacked the will and power for righteousness, even
where society's requirements were far less rigorous than
God's commands. The believers' great service to Western
civilization was that, amid pagan culture miring in its shame,
they reflected the higher righteousness that God requires
as an approximated reality in life. This the believers did,
moreover, with a joy that disarmed the exponents and de-
votees of sin.

The early Christians knew that they were sent to the
ends of this earth within this earth's history. Their spiritual
vision of the cosmos under Christ and of government under
God, and their proclamation of Jahweh's justice and of
Jesus' justification provided essential perspective and power;
loss in recent times of that perspective and power explains
much of the plight of the modern nations.

5. It takes some boldness to venture what the early
Christians would have done in today's circumstances. And if
we ask what we modern Christians might have done in their
circumstances, insofar as we might have changed loyalties and
convictions, it is quite possible we would have imposed upon
New Testament Christianity the very weaknesses which
plague the church in the twentieth century. We have a global
wealth that the early Christians lacked and a world-wisdom
that they disclaimed. And although the church now has little
world-power of a political sort, however much some bureau-
crats aspire to it, the religious hierarchies nevertheless repre-
sent vast ecclesiastical establishments measured even by
the yardstick of Big Business. For all that, we do not have,
indeed we clearly lack what early Christianity had, namely,
steadfast continuance in the apostles' doctrine and fellowship

in prayer and in breaking of bread (Acts 4:42) — and all this in a context, moreover, in which God worked wonders that overawed both church and world.

If we cannot outline in detail what the early Christians might do among us today, nevertheless certain verities can be confidently affirmed. Were the early Christians with us now, they would still speak as men stunned by Christ's crucifixion but shocked alive by his resurrection. The voice that declared "I am he that liveth and was dead" (Rev. 1:18) they recognized and obeyed. Were they among us now those early Christians would still know themselves as loosed from their sins by the Saviour's shed blood (Rev. 1:5), and as enlivened by the Spirit of holiness. They would exhibit a new personality alive to the eternal world, a personality on speaking terms with God, in fellowship with the Risen Head of the Church, indwelt by the Holy Spirit, incorporated into the divine redemptive-covenant, and expectant of the Lord's return. But they would insist, for all that, on the indispensability of their world-wide task, namely, evangelization of the earth and gathering of a new family whose very diversity of membership attests the cosmopolitan nature of Christ's church. They would admit the complexity of problems in a world so largely given over to the Evil One. But they would be neither dismayed nor deterred by what so many modern churchmen consider an occasion for replacing reliance on Christ and the gospel with a resort to Caesar and to silver and gold to solve society's deepest need. Nor would the early Christians think the evangelistic mandate superseded and futile because of the scientific revolution, technological breakthrough or burgeoning population. Remembering that their own proportions were once eleven souls against the whole world, they would not become defensive because of a multiplying majority of non-Christians. More than that, they would remember that whether men be few or many, any who remain strangers to grace are doomed to a debased destiny, an existence outside of Christ which can be but a living death.

Amid the technological breakthrough and a cybernetic age that seem to have depersonalized man, we can hear the early Christians entreating us to use rather than deplore this staggering technology. As never before we can literally tell the whole world not simply the most recent tragedies of unregenerate existence but first and foremost the secret of new being. Man in the pre-industrial era was no more fully human than man in our cybernetic age. In regeneration alone lies his rehumanization; the old life, at whatever stage in history, and even at its best, is subpersonal. Recognizing that the problem of the assembly line is indeed a serious concern of Christian ethics, the early Christians would have wrestled with its implications. But they would have insisted as well that men alive only to things and dead to God are but half-men; they would have declared "Christ in you" to be man's only hope of glory even in this cybernetic century.

For the first Christians the spectacular successes of modern science — its deadly power to blast cities off the map, as well as its exploratory propulsion of missiles and men to the moon — would not have lessened the power (the *dunamis*) of the gospel. They knew that Jesus' power over death and his moral power over sin is incomparable, unique, and beyond human manufacture and manipulation. As men who once cowered in the presence of the grave they now walked willingly through martyrdom into the arms of the Risen One; men once ethically defeated now not only lived godly lives but also carried in their hearts the moral fortunes of all mankind.

Were these New Testament Christians among us, nothing in modern society would deter them from the boldest of initiatives for the Good News. To the many unconvincing excuses that modern Christians offer for silence or equivocation in the Christian mission, these early Christians would have countered with the one and the only one valid reason for urgency in declaring the gospel: God had spoken, Christ had died and risen, and man otherwise doomed in sin can even now have the life divinely intended for the human species and alone fit for time and eternity.

The Truth 4
of the Gospel

People used to say "it's the gospel truth" to guarantee the incontrovertible factuality of their statements. But in our time the truth of the gospel has been so attacked and assailed that many moderns question the validity of the gospel-truth itself. Not a few, in fact, assert the relativity of all truth; indeed, the very truth of truth is questioned.

Such double loss of the gospel's truth and of all truth — as an objective and transcendent claim upon the human mind—is an unmistakable facet of the civilizational crisis that has engulfed modern Western culture. Central to this crisis of truth is the modern eclipse of God together with the consequent forfeiture of the revelation of truth and the truth of revelation.

Even pagan philosophers like Plato in pre-Christian times knew that to speak of truth rather than of opinion is to delve inevitably into the invisible spiritual world. It was erroneous of classical philosophers to seek a changeless truth independently of God, and equally so to locate it immanently in the supposedly divine universal reason of mankind. But through two thousand years of Western history their awareness still holds true that the changing space-time world can neither supply any unchanging truth nor establish any enduring moral norms.

On becoming a Christian the great philosopher Augustine

recognized that no truth exists independently of God — that God himself is the Truth, and that enduring truth is identical with the very mind of God. The probing of truth, as Augustine realized, is in the last instance nothing other than probing the revelation of the true and living God.

God's very existence, and with this the objectivity of truth, have been submerged, alas, in tidal waves of modern doubt. The spiritual crisis of mankind is also an intellectual crisis, inasmuch as the modern temper is now disposed to consider God unthinkable, unchanging truth an illusion and gospel-truth a fiction. Truth itself seems at times to have gone to the Devil, and the planet Earth to have become a cosmic Tower of Babel.

Some weeks ago while grading a stack of true-false examination papers I suddenly discovered a costly mistake. I had dozed off just long enough to misplace the master key, and had begun marking papers routinely by an uncorrected student exam. With a start I realized I was correcting the master key on the basis of the fallible student paper. What a parable of the thought-world of our day! Abandoning an objective norm of truth, it relies on a fallible guide, and then dares even to conform the Law and Gospel of God to some human alternatives.

Today the whole field of truth is on the defensive. Multitudes of people are gripped by totalitarian lies, snared by commercial slogans and popular clichés, entranced by vogue-ideas and warped words. It is fashionable to be committed to scientific revisability, resigned to the historical character of all man's knowledge, fascinated with evolutionary development, reliant upon empirical method, devoted to dialectical paradox, preoccupied with existential decision, and derisive of God-talk.

Swept along by this tide, and contributing to it as well, neo-Protestant theologians have emphasized trust more than truth; minimizing the intellectual context and content of Christian decision, they have devalued the logic of Christian commitment. In the aftermath of Kant's distortion of the limits of human reason and his disallowance of divine revelation, more recent theology, although reinstating the revelational reality of God, has nonetheless retained man's cognitive vacuity about God. That we have no knowledge of God as he objectively exists despite his disclosure, and that we can make no universally valid statements about his nature and purpose, was already a misguided tenet of Ritschlian, Barthian and Bultmannian theology long before it stirred American death-of-God theologians to lay God-talk to rest. This ruling dogma of God's conceptual inaccessibility unfortunately cancelled out the only convincing reply to logical positivism's unjustifiable claim that the empirical methodology of contemporary science annuls the truth-status of metaphysical assertions.

Nothing is more foundationally important for the world and for the church in the twentieth century than a recovery of truth. Truth-famine is the ultimate and worst of all famines. Unless modern culture recovers the truth of truth and the truth of God, civilization is doomed to oblivion and the spirit of man to nihilism.

Let me comment briefly, then, on the divinity of the truth, the demonstration of the truth, and the destination of the truth.

I. The Divinity of the Gospel Truth

In *The Decline and Fall of the Roman Empire,* Edward Gibbon remarked that "the various modes of worship which prevailed in the Roman world were all considered by the people as equally true, by the philosophers as equally false, and by the magistrates as equally useful." Today's magistrates, especially those who cope with vexing church-state problems, consider religion a nuisance, whereas politicians often find religion useful. Marxists, as we know, label religion an opiate and supernaturalism an illusion. For multitudes of people, in fact, any and all religions have now become equally optional or superfluous. As for philosophers, many of them skirt the question of religion's truth or falsity and stress instead its psychological function.

The issue of the truth or falsity of religion is far more obscured today than ever it was in the ancient pagan world. And contributing to this climate of uncertainty and indifference over the truth of religion has been recent neo-Protestant theology. To say, as it does, that Christianity is unique is not enough — every religion has distinctives. Nor is it enough to call the Christian religion redemptive — most religions have inner consequences of one sort or another.

The church's good tidings mean little apart from the ultimate truth of revealed religion. "We are in grave danger of forgetting," David H. C. Read has said, and he is right, "that the first question about any religion is not whether or not it is useful, but whether or not it is *true*" (*I Am Persuaded,* New York: Charles Scribner's Sons, 1961, p. 58).

Only on the basis of God's self-revelation and self-declaration can we speak confidently and authoritatively about God. Indeed, if we know anything whatever not subject to change, anything fixed and final, anything absolutely true, it will be so not as a fruit of scientific investigation, which always invites revision, nor as a by-product of incomplete and enlarging human experience, but solely in view of a Word of God.

In an age surfeited with words and surmises we need to be startled and summoned by the special force of Jesus Christ's double Amen: "In truth, in very truth I tell you . . . !" In contrast with modern Christian and ancient Jewish usage of the term to ratify someone else's assertion, Jesus, as Ernst Käsemann reminds us, used the Amen for declarations that were his very own, and by way of introducing his sayings. He doubled this introductory Amen, moreover, to emphasize the divine authority and truth of his own Word: "Amen, Amen, I say unto you!" He affirmed direct knowledge of the

Father (Matt. 11:27) and claimed to unveil the very mind and will of God (John 5:19 f.). "He that sent me is true," he declared, "and I speak to the world those things which I have heard of him" (John 8:26).

Biblical Christianity demands uncompromising centrality for the living God who speaks and shows, for the divine revelation of the truth, for God's universal disclosure in nature, history and conscience, and for his special disclosure in prophetic-apostolic Scripture and supremely in the incarnate Word Jesus Christ. Evangelical theism, therefore, should boldly take the field today to champion the cause of truth in its proclamation of God's grace.

Christianity calls men to decision on the basis of truth that is valid at one and the same time for unlettered multitudes and erudite philosophers, for the wisest magistrates and the most powerful politicians. Paul proclaimed the Creator-Redeemer God to quarreling philosophers in Athens; Peter and John ignored repressive rulers to expound the gospel-truth. The apostles' evangelistic target for the gospel was nothing less than the whole world and all mankind. They knew that the truth of truth, the truth of God, and the truth of the gospel stand or fall together.

The God of the Bible summons men everywhere to worship him in spirit and in truth. As the illuminating light of men, the Logos preserves us before this God in responsible, rational, moral and spiritual relationships. God intends to etch his ineradicable truth on every human heart: "The covenant I will make . . . , says the Lord, is this: I will put my laws in their minds and write them on their hearts. . . . All of them, high and low, shall know me" (Heb. 8:10 ff.).

The heathen, says Paul, exchanged the truth of God for a lie, and "bartered away the true God for a false one" (Rom. 1:25, New English Bible). Renouncing the revelation of God that "makes for life and true religion" (II Peter 1:3, N.E.B.), they inherited not only bogus divinities but also "misguided minds . . . plunged in darkness" and a way of reasoning that

deadends in futility (Rom. 1:21). That such a world,
"heathen at heart and deaf to the truth" (Acts 7:51), might
know God's truth and the gospel-truth the Church was
founded and scattered abroad. The message of Christianity
is no mixture of magic and myth; it unmasks the difference
between truth and fiction. "This is in truth the Saviour of
the world" (John 4:42) declare the Samaritans when they
hear Jesus for themselves. Paul writes the Ephesians: "You
. . . heard the message of the truth, the good news of your
salvation, and . . . believed it" (Eph. 1:13, N.E.B.).

Centrally at stake in the gospel is the God of truth and the
truth of God. Christian truth is not some special slice of
coherence, or some preferred segment of truth as a whole.
By Christian truth we mean, rather, the whole truth, the
entirety of truth grounded in the eternal Logos, truth as the
Divine Mind gives it to men to know, as the inspired Scriptures report it, and as the incarnate Logos unveils it. Christian truth is *veritas* insofar as the revelation of God has en-
abled men to know the truth. "True life" (Luke 21:19), "true
justice" (James 3:18), "true faith" (I Tim. 2:7), "true doctrine" (Titus 1:9), "teaching the truth" (II Tim. 3:16),
taking "firm hold on the deep truth of our faith" (I Tim.
3:9) are familiar themes of the New Testament. Truth is an
essential part of the Christian armor; to meditate on "all that
is true" (Phil. 4:8, N.E.B.) is a part of the Christian's calling.
The power of this truth is what the church proffers to a
doomed and decadent world. On this powerful truth sus-
pends all the integrity of the Christian message, and among
its indispensable concerns are the self-disclosure of the true
and living God, the intelligibility of divine revelation, the
rationality of Christian belief, and the logic of Christian
commitment.

The gospel-truth is in no sense man's invention but in
every regard is fully and only God's disclosure. Would any
human religion portray God so holy and man so renegade
that self-rescue by human ingenuity and works is totally im-

possible? No human philosophy has ever declared that the supernatural God promised an historical redemption, chose an insignificant nation for a witness to the world, became incarnate in the Babe of Bethlehem, vanquished death in the resurrection of Jesus and vindicated the Crucified and Risen One as the firstfruits of a universal resurrection of the dead. In the incarnation and victory of the Truth incarnate, in Jesus Christ who fulfills the prophetic vision of mercy and truth embracing each other (Ps. 85:10) and who is himself "full of grace and truth" (John 1:14), the divinity of the Truth soars to its revelational summit.

Now especially when the gospel-truth is in every way so crucial for contemporary man, we are called anew to the witness stand. "Stand by the truth you have learned" (II Tim. 3:14) Paul exhorts his spiritual son Timothy, and from the Mamertine prison writes to the Philippian Christians: "When I appear . . . in the dock to vouch for the truth of the Gospel, you all share in the privilege that is mine" (Phil. 1:7, N.E.B.). Demanding recognition of the truth of truth and of its divinity, Christianity calls mankind to account before the truth and law of God. The divinity of truth means that men are confronted daily, in the realm of mind and will with the possibility of contradicting the Logos. For a generation aware that reason is an instrument for knowing the truth of God, truth is a life-or-death matter. The truth of God spurned and the law of God violated underlie man's universal sinfulness and his need for redemption. Calling man to behold the Truth-incarnate, the gospel proposes to open man's spirit anew to the transcendent Logos, to anchor man's soul firmly to the True and Living God, to station the creature once again beneath his Creator in obedience to the Word of God. God's truth forces sinful man to a choice either of contradicting the Cosmic Christ and crucifying Jesus of Nazareth, or of accepting and following the incarnate Logos even through martyrdom to Truth's eternal home.

This alternative is thrust no less upon men of our time than upon those of previous generations.

II. The Demonstration of the Gospel-Truth

The truth of the gospel is demonstrated in resurrection-might, as well as by its power of logical conviction. The historical resurrection of the crucified Jesus from the dead, the present spiritual regeneration of God's twice-born children, and the coming final resurrection of all mankind to a two-fold destiny in eternity all attest to its awesome truth.

According to Samuel H. Moffett, the indispensable word for the evangel today is *power:* "Not black power, or student power, or flower power, but God power" ("What Is the Evangel?," *Christianity Today,* March 13, 1970, p. 3). Paul writes to the Corinthians of "the attested truth of God . . . Christ nailed to the cross . . . not . . . subtle arguments . . . . The Gospel . . . carried conviction by spiritual powers," he adds, "so that your faith might be built not upon human wisdom but upon the power of God" (I Cor. 2:1-5). Through the apostle's pivotal declaration that "Christ died for our sins according to the scriptures, and was buried, and rose again the third day according to the scriptures, and was seen . . . ." (I Cor. 15:3-4) we catch the essence of the earliest preaching of the primitive missionary churches.

The truth of revelation is no speculative *gnosis* or man-made philosophy. Even as revelation, God's truth is something intended not simply to be known, but something also to be done. To abstract it from its potency in life is no victory for gospel-truth, for God's Word has an event-character.

The gospel is God's *dunamis* unto salvation, and no modern dynamite can match its might. More potent than all the fulminations of totalitarian tyrants, than all the weaponry of atomic warfare, the God of Truth brings the Crucified

Jesus to life and, to replace a created world that fallen man has ruined, calls into being a new heavens and earth.

Jesus Christ is the Truth of God's supreme demonstration. Not alone in prophecy do we see the end-time image that the redeemed are to bear, not simply in Scripture is God's new covenant sketched upon the heart of man, but in Jesus of Nazareth divine sonship is already mirrored in the midst of human history. The event of Jesus Christ is the demonstrated Truth that shatters the reign of sin and portrays human nature in the glad spiritual service of man's holy Maker. Jesus of Nazareth who "went about doing good" (Acts 10:38) is the Truth of God enfleshed. He is the Truth who suffered contradiction of sinners, the Truth indestructible even on the Cross, the Truth towering still over sin and death and hell and the Devil, the crucified and vindicated Logos, the True and Living Word.

It should come as no surprise that the modern relativizing of truth and a lessened respect for verbal forms go hand in hand. Having accepted the relativity of truth, contemporary man is increasingly resigned to the vanity of words. He shows a high preference for nonverbal media and finds wholly private meanings in today's art forms. In *Waiting for Godot* Samuel Beckett ventures telling the whole story without a single word. Music and the arts no longer communicate the shared experience of common values. To the extent that television and radio project mostly images, sounds and emotions, to that extent do they reflect this growing revolt against universally valid meaning. A mass media cult of nonverbal experience would demote and trivialize the whole cultural inheritance of the West.

More revealing of our times however, is the further notion that words, rather than being a revelation of the truth, are, in fact, only a refuge; indeed, they are considered likely to distort and even to deceive. This growing modern feeling that words are no longer trustworthy bearers of truth is a direct corollary and consequence of anti-intellectual and existential theories of life and has serious implications for a theology of the revealed Word of God.

To hope that nonverbal experience will remedy spiritual emptiness is predictably futile. Deverbalizing an already depersonalized society will only worsen matters, for man will then be all the more dehumanized. Muteness is no improvement over the human hubbub and world Babel; it is a decline, in fact, toward the subhuman.

Unfortunately a number of evangelical Christians respond to this cult of the nonverbal by stigmatizing television and radio as radically evil. Obviously no one would consider the mass media exempt from the contamination spawned by man's fall and fallibility. And reasons for levelling specially harsh judgment on the media are not hard to find. At times news coverage seems to pursue the deviant out of all proportion; historic Christian faith is devalued if not overlooked and religious discussion sometimes denies evangelical Christianity equal time or representation. But is this situation inevitable in mass media communication? And are the mass media wholly to blame? The fact is that in using the media evangelical Christianity is too much trapped in American subculture and too little involved in frontier dialogue. Even where it enjoys mass media opportunities, it is often naive about addressing the secular mood, and talks largely to or at those already evangelically aligned.

Today's concern with the contemporary scene condemns the media to covering predominantly bad news. It becomes easy, then, to conclude that the media are hostile to good news and in the service of what is bad. The conclusion that needs to be drawn, rather, is that the good news affirmed by Christianity requires visibility no less than audibility; in a mass-media age it is imperative to demonstrate as well as declare the gospel-truth.

To brand the media *per se* as intrinsically distortive and necessarily antagonistic to the truth is a serious error, one that encourages inexcusable distrust moreover, and costly

neglect by evangelicals of these very media. If words are
essentially untrustworthy — or become so when communi-
cated by the mass media — then there will be little future
in a technological civilization for the truth of revelation and
the preaching of the gospel. Biblical Christianity can afford
neither a nonverbal nor anti-mass-media approach to life.

There is, however, a legitimate complaint to be made
over words, and evangelical Christianity, in view of its
spiritual heritage, cannot afford to suppress it.

Proclamation of the gospel-truth is doomed unless pulsat-
ing life renders the spoken and written word potent even
before it is preached. A hallmark of Biblical Christianity
is its irreducible distinction between a dead orthodoxy con-
sisting only in words and a living breathing faith. Dead
orthodoxy by unwittingly encouraging the secular notion
that words are but a front and a fakery, bestows a diminish-
ing power upon the spiritual word. Truth and word then
become associated with God while life is associated with
sham. The demand to strip away mere verbiage so that
men may perceive spiritual reality and moral power is inherent in the Biblical call for demonstration of the truth.
Knowing that word and deed together are revelatory of
the truth of God, evangelical Christianity should and must
sound this demand. To rob the Word and words as well
of their role as agent and medium of revelation is to undercut the intelligibility of revelation, to obscure the Word of
Truth, frustrate the truth of the Word, and encourage the
notion that words are inherently untrustworthy, and the gospel as such merely a matter of prescribed words and
formulas.

What then of our manifested sonship in and to the world?
What of our daily demonstration of the gospel-truth? Only
the gospel-truth demonstrated can fully expose the counter-
feit character of what often passes for truth in thought and
word, but is devoid of Biblical love and justice, holiness and
joy. "Of course we all 'have knowledge,'" writes Paul, who

can even disdain knowledge that "breeds conceit." "It is love that builds," he adds, and whoever fancies he has knowledge apart from love "knows nothing yet, in the true sense of knowing" (I Cor. 8:2, New English Bible). To the Ephesians Paul wrote: "Let us speak the truth in love; so shall we fully grow up into Christ" (Eph. 4:14 f.). John similarly proclaims love to be the evidence and manifestation of the truth: "he that loveth not, knoweth not God" (I John 3:8, cf. 3:19). Lovelessness, he adds, gives the lie to our words (I John 4:20); it clouds rather than commends the divinity of the truth.

Paul further exhorted the Ephesians, "Give up living like pagans with their good-for-nothing notions. Their wits are beclouded, they are strangers to the life that is in God, because ignorance prevails among them and their minds have grown hard as stone . . . and [they] stop at nothing to satisfy their foul desires. But . . . were you not as Christians taught the truth as it is in Jesus? — that, leaving your former way of life, you must lay aside that old human nature which, deluded by its lusts, is sinking towards death. You must be made new in mind and spirit, and put on the new nature of God's creating, which shows itself in the just and devout life called for by the truth" (Eph. 4:17-24, N.E.B.).

Such demonstration manifests and proves the transcendent power of the gospel-truth. All who believe, it lifts to a new order of existence in the midst of human history, shaping them into a new race of men who reflect the fellowship of the twice-born in a new society, and who exhibit the standards of the Kingdom of God. Paul writes to the Corinthians: "When anyone is united to Christ, there is a new world; the old order has gone, and a new order has already begun" (II Cor. 5:17, N.E.B.). "In you," he tells the Corinthian converts, "the evidence for the truth of Christ has found confirmation" (I Cor. 1:6, N.E.B.). The truth of the evangel is not merely a series of verbal propositions to be repeated in the right way at the right time and place before the right people; it is an enduring truth for perpetual living before all men. When God seeks and rescues lost and doomed sinners from the penalty, guilt and power of sin, he restores them to spiritual fellowship with himself and to holiness. "God who said, 'Out of darkness let light shine,' has caused his light to shine within us, to give the light of revelation — the revelation of the glory of God in the face of Jesus Christ" (II Cor. 4:6, N.E.B.).

III. The Destination of the Gospel-Truth

Where does the truth lead? Where will it take us? The logic of life no less than the logic of the schools looks for a final outcome and conclusion.

Pragmatists have long told us that only what works is true. While Christianity holds aloft its own banner for good works together with saving grace, it totally disavows such speculative weakness-riddled philosophy. The Christian religion affirms not simply that "the gospel is true because it works," but rather and as prior that "the gospel works because it is true." Originating in eternity the gospel's truth and power also find a destination in eternity. The gospel-truth leads "home," as many a hymnwriter has noted; it escorts sinners in this present life to redemptive rescue, and will finally usher the redeemed into the very presence of the Father. "I am the Way," said Jesus — the Way to the Father, that is — "no man cometh to the Father but by me" (John 14:6).

False gospels deceive and defraud, demote and degrade, and dead-end in disillusion and dishonor. Unfortunately they are not merely harmless daydreams, but deepen man's degeneracy, and lead him astray and away from redemption and regeneration. Doomed to fail, however, all such deceptions and distortions will be exposed at last in their deviltry rather than divinity, and be brought to judgment before the holy God.

Only a church gone worldly and apostate will put aside the question of last things. Interestingly enough secular scientists and movie-producers in our day are making apocalyptic motifs of the Bible a special concern. Scientists warn constantly against the possibilities of a man-made cosmic end-time, whether through atomic destruction or global pollution. A Harvard professor has escalated the accelerating odds for full scale nuclear war to one chance in three by 1990, and one chance in two by the year 2000. According to some ecologists extinction by pollution may come even sooner.

Meanwhile the movie-men use the world's impending demise to make sport and to make money. Joseph Morgenstern, general editor of *Newsweek,* says that "it doesn't take much to get with the spirit of apocalypse these days" because "we know . . . things can't go on much longer as they're going, and the prospect of a climax to the whole human drama has its deadly fascination." "Never before," he comments, "have the merchandisers of movies been so high on the commercial potential of extinction" ("Bang! Apocalypse for Sale," April 27, 1970 issue, p. 97).

That these people attach a cash value to the end-time motif betrays a mentality sadly and tragically warped to the truth of the gospel. Eschatological entertainment carries no implication whatever that modern man is softening his heart to the God of the final future; rather, such pastime seems to steel the secular spirit against the truth and word of revelation. The word which modern man elsewhere relativizes and rejects for the nonverbal is here revived but revived naked of revelational value. If no authoritative word remains today, then neither is there any final eschatological word to be uttered. When the word is denied any role in divine judgment, by the same token it is deprived of any liberating force.

Apocalyptic entertainment vacates the Truth of God and the Word of God before they are even heard, and by thus cutting the message of judgment and grace unwittingly reserves for modern man a front seat at God's final judgment. As Morgenstern remarks, the cinematic experts "keep playing with an apocalypse from which there can be no possible renaissance" (ibid., p. 98). Even before the last trump has sounded, they seal the final future and replace the Biblical hope by non-providential fate.

Despite such sacrilege the destination of the Truth and Word of God is as sure as their divinity and demonstration. By the Word of God preexistent, God created the heavens and the earth (John 1:3); by the Word of God incarnate he redeemed a fallen race (John 1:14); by the Word of God risen and exalted he will execute his final judgment (Rev. 19:13). "Behold a white horse; and he that sat upon him was called Faithful and True and in righteousness he doth judge and make war. . . . And he was clothed with a vesture dipped in blood: and his name is called The Word of God" (Rev. 19:13). Acknowledged by the gospel-truth as the divine agent and executive in the coming judgment is the Living Word of God.

Communists speak of the inevitable triumph of the proletariat; social radicals talk about inevitable world revolution. Others predict inevitable global atomic war, still others speak of an inevitable decline of all the great Western powers or of an inevitable economic collapse. But there is only one real inevitability: it is necessary that the Scripture be fulfilled. The Word of God cannot be bound.

The outcome of God's truth in the future is absolutely dependable as in the present and past. In his first advent Jesus of Nazareth fulfilled the inspired prophecies. "This text . . . had to come true," writes John (15:25). Again and again we are told "the text of Scripture came true" (John 19:25). "This prophecy in Scripture was bound to come true" writes Luke (Acts 1:16). Elsewhere he quotes Jesus: "In your hearing this text has come true" (Luke 4:21), and that what was "written by the prophets will come true for

the Son of Man" (Luke 18:31). Likewise in the coming
future the prophetic word, the truth of God, is sure. Of
God's final trumpet call the apostle Paul writes: "The saying of Scripture will come true" (I Cor. 15:54).

We read in the Acts of the Apostles that the comman-
dant of the Roman troops in Jerusalem "could not get at
the truth because of the hubbub" (Acts 21:34, N.E.B.).
A riot was in progress, stirred by fellow Jews who accused
the apostle Paul of spreading Christian doctrine over the
wide world and who demanded his death (Acts 21:28, 31).
Even amid that tumult we find the great Apostle bearing
his ready witness to the gospel truth. So, too, we are called
to reflect its high claim to a world in deepening darkness,
a world which considers truth abstruse and words obscure;
to a world that so lumps experience into a cacophony of
sounds, images and emotions that men dare to toy with the
holy theme of apocalypse. Not only for the movie-makers
and for mass media but for the whole twentieth century
world, truth and word hang in the balances. As never
before we need sound and sight for the revelation of Scripture. Here alone are to be found a worthy life-view, a
coherent world-view, a joyful end-view. Only the truth
of God centering in the gospel-truth, and the gospel-truth
as the whole counsel of God, can restore worth to life and
life to worth.

While the day of decision remains, the church of Christ
must in life and word be the global echo of the Risen
Christ's invitation to turn from judgment to joy. This address to the world is not only in audible words, but also in
a compassionate demonstration of the gospel truth; enfleshed
goodness and justice are the church's special fashion, a style
of life that mirrors heaven as her proximate abode. "We
come therefore as Christ's ambassadors. . . . For our sake
God made him one with the sinfulness of men, so that we
might be made one with the goodness of God himself.
Sharing in God's work, we urge this appeal upon you. . . ."

(II Cor. 5:20 ff., N.E.B.). In authentic Christian living the gospel-truth shimmers already with an earnest of resurrection realities, with an approximation of the moral image of Jesus Christ, and with a sample of our final inheritance. The church best brings the world under harassing fire of the age to come not simply by its faithful preaching of the gospel, and a warning of the penalties of neglect, but also by the advance commitment of her own energies under the sway of the Coming King, and an exhibition of the rewards of obedience.

Upon us as believers the divinity of the gospel-truth, the demonstration of the gospel-truth, and the destination of the gospel-truth places the burden, the opportunity and the privilege and entrustment of facing the world with the Word. Let us do so in a way that makes decision for Christ not an unintelligible noise or an easy evasion, but a welcome option and unparalleled opportunity.

The Theology 5
of Revolution

The history of the twentieth century has been one of political discontent and accelerating revolution. Global manifestations of riot, revolt and rebellion have become routine items of each day's world news. Erstwhile centers of democracy show a declining confidence in reason and law, and suffer increasing reliance on coercion and force as the accepted dynamic for social change. Totalitarian tyrants have imposed restrictive regimes by means of violence, and in many lands indignant masses now aspire in vain to overthrow them by sudden counterforce. Where the *status quo* still prevails, resentful nations turn to revolutionary allies for hopeful and swift inversion of their plight.

What has evangelical Christianity to say to this revolutionary temper in a critically rebellious world situation? The Christian vanguard must assess the presuppositions and propriety of this radical approach to the problems of society because revolution is almost always moralized as a necessary means of curtailing or ending unbearable injustices. The theology of revolution recently has emerged in neo-Protestant circles to provide a supposedly Christian rationale for the forced overthrow of unjust social structures. Is the widening contemporary revolt against inherited authority, structures and institutions to be considered a reflection of the fall of man, or an evidence of evolutionary progress, or a legitimate and even distinctively Christian means of social redemption?

The Biblical view exposes the whole of human history to God's searching and searing judgment. The Decalogue sweeps both individual and social relationships into its commanding purview, and the stern prophetic warnings remind us that unrighteousness pervades man's social life no less than his personal life and brings into sharp focus God's displeasure over a distressing range of public iniquity and social injustice.

This prophetic emphasis on Yahweh's universal reign and righteous demand contrasts markedly with the limited claims made for merely national and tribal gods of the ancient religious world. No less irreducibly unique is the prophetic vision and expectation of a coming kingdom of social righteousness and world peace. The Biblical view supplies the ultimate source of our modern expectations of a utopian climax of history, whereas elsewhere in the ancient world religious and philosophical theory located history's golden age only in the remote past, or viewed ongoing history as cyclical.

To be sure, the prevalent modern vision of global peace and justice differs in important respects from Biblically-defined expectations. The prophetic-apostolic view is inherently messianic; that is, it is mediated by God's anointed agent, especially through the redemptive presence and powerful reign of the Divine Redeemer. The ideals of the Kingdom, moreover, are spiritual and moral, centering in God's reign over an obedient people responsive to his holy will; the Kingdom is not concentrated simply in external social structures and statutory legislation independently of man's good will. While the New Covenant cannot be depicted as disinterested in just social legislation and structures, the Kingdom of God has transcendent eschatological and spiritual-moral features absent from secular utopian expectations.

The use of force to implement social justice, an emphasis standing in the forefront of the theology of revolution, has a surface affinity with the Biblical teaching that in this present fallen world God sanctions coercive authority to restrain evil and disorder and to promote justice and peace. To assign force a legitimate role in securing justice recognizes that social and political problems are more complex than mere individual or neighbor-relationships. Love is not in a fallen society an adequate dynamic for resolving all human problems, particularly not for problems of public life. Contrary to pacifist theory which stipulates that love is the only authentic presupposition of Christian ethics and alone constitutes a proper response to evil, the New Testament approves a just use of power in the public realm alongside an ethic of love in personal neighbor-relationships. To repudiate all use of physical force in a fallen society is less than moral.

Yet the correlation of force and justice espoused by the theology of revolution differs in fundamental respects from the Biblical emphasis on civil authority as the divinely sanctioned instrumentality for promoting justice in society. In the Bible God sanctions civil government as the divinely approved framework for the public containment of disorder and injustice and for the advancement of justice and order. But the theology of revolution promotes civil disobedience and advocates the forced overthrow of established government as the ideal means of social change.

While the theology of pacifism oversimplifies the social crisis by viewing neighbor-relationships as basically determinative of human history, the theology of revolution errs by viewing socio-political structures as finally determinative. The pacifist theologian will be tempted to charge the evangelical non-pacifist with a damaging concession to revolutionary theology because of the willingness to justify war as a legitimate moral response, while the evangelical non-pacifist will be tempted to charge the pacifist with unwittingly preparing the way for revolutionary theology through over-simplification of the realm of corporate political action to the dimensions of interpersonal love-relationships. Both, however, repudiate as immoral the use of violence, whether in the name of the church or not, to overthrow existing socio-political institutions and to force Kingdom-principles or politico-economic options upon the world at large.

In general, evangelical Christianity acknowledges that social structures exert vast power in the public arena and carry staggering influence either for good or evil. But new institutions cannot of themselves guarantee a better society where old life-styles remain. Civil justice requires only outward conformity to law, but does not require personal reconciliation or changed motives, but goodwill takes precedence over structures. Hence evangelical Christianity insists that man's goodwill is even more fundamental than external structures and that a new heart is indispensable for realizing any approximately ideal society in a fallen world. Good men will resist and transcend unjust structures.

Evangelical Christianity holds that human history and culture are everywhere under divine judgment, and that God is everywhere active in history either in judgment or in redemption. Hence it shares in any and every searching critique of the *status quo*. Anywhere and everywhere it must challenge injustice in the divine name, recalling man and society to the righteousness of God.

The radical secular theologians tell us that God is today speaking in revolution, that is, at the frontiers of social ferment and political change in modern history, and they exhort the Christian church to identify itself boldly with revolutionary assault upon the past. Radical or revolutionary theology gains its distinctive character, and sets itself in opposition to evangelical social ethics, through three peculiar emphases: first, that existing social orders are beyond evangelical rectification as instruments of justice and peace; second, that Christians should and must use whatever force is necessary to change these existing orders; and third, that revolutionary overthrow of existing structures will inaugurate a just society. These tenets when assessed in Biblical perspective are so questionable that the Christian rightness of the so-called theology of revolution must stand in serious doubt.

The radical judgment of the theology of revolution upon existing social structures rests upon a badly distorted and highly ambiguous view of sin. On the other hand, its estimate of sin is grossly exaggerated, or it could not consider existing social structures now so warped by injustice and so alien to God's purpose in creation that they are wholly beyond present serviceability or hope of renewal, and therefore in need of forceful replacement by a socially-conscientious vanguard. It considers injustice so deeply pervasive of history that nothing short of revolution can now remedy the plight of humanity. The orders of creation are therefore thought to be so warped by sin that they are no longer amenable to divine renewal or serviceable to justice, and instead require immediate and forced replacement.

If this is true then society is victimized by evil far more pervasively than even the Bible indicates. If social structures in the presently fallen world are beyond any and all possible serviceability as a framework for the achievement of public righteousness, then the fall and its consequences have despoiled the created orders far more ruinously than Biblical theology concedes.

But the fact is that Scripture points to civil government as the responsible tool for justice, and not to the radical secular alternative of coercive revolution. According to the New Testament, civil government is God's stipulated instrument for preserving social justice and public order in fallen human history. Although political authority is capable of abuse and being abused, it is divinely responsible for social justice and order, and supplies the most ideal framework for their public preservation in this fallen world.

To assert the irremedial corruption of all historical institutions and to imply, as any thorough-going theory of revo-
tion must, the dispensability of even divinely-willed orders
of creation and preservation, is therefore to cast aside the
very framework within which justice and order are hope-
fully attainable.

Were the orders of creation and preservation actually
in such dire straits as this revolutionary perspective implies,
it would be highly questionable whether any effort by fallen
man, however concerted and powerful, could effectively
replace them by preferable historical alternatives. Were the
orders of creation and preservation as convulsed and de-
formed as the theology of revolution suggests, nothing could
arrest the total collapse of human civilization. By its exces-
sive pessimism over existing structures, and by forfeiting all
possibilities of their renewal as instrumentalities of justice,
the theology of revolution, whatever may be its intentions,
invites and promotes nothing less than social anarchy. A
revolutionary approach to the framework for securing social
change may sooner or later dispense with the divinely
established correlation of sex with monogamous marriage
and of economic reward with labor, as well as of social
justice with civil government. While the theology of revolution may regard the disruption of existing institutions as
a means to an end, its assault on modern society actually
becomes an unwitting end-in-itself of the revolutionary
spirit.

Secular theories of social ethics grant the Christian doc-
trines of creation and preservation no decisive historical
significance over against evolutionary development and
therefore readily relativize both the past and the present.
Such evolutionary theory has exerted marked influence even
upon contemporary expositions of Christian social ethics.
For instance, despite his insistence on the centrality of the
resurrection of the Crucified Jesus, on the Kingdom of God
as a divine accomplishment, and on the indispensability of

divine regeneration, Jürgen Moltmann, in his eschato-
logically-oriented theology of hope, so dispenses with any
fixed role for divinely created orders that evolutionary dy-
namics shape much of the conscious course of history. For
Moltmann, the notion of *provolution* supersedes that of *regeneration* in social ethics.

If the theology of revolution in some ways grossly exag-
gerates the sway of sin in history, in other respects it holds
a feeble and unrealistic view of sin, since it apparently
believes that revolution can and will presently usher in an
ideal society. The revolutionary fervor is blind to its own
inherent limitations and uncritical of its pretensions to incarnate the spirit of justice. The Biblical revelation recognizes
that evil is more thoroughgoing and penetrating: it denies
the possibility of secular utopia in fallen history; it sees in
spiritual regeneration the only present dynamic for realizing
an approximately just society on earth; it connects the structures and statutes necessary to public justice with the social
commandments of God; it calls revolutionary activists and
revolutionary societies no less than others to repentance and
divine renewal; and it warns that the Lord of History will
in his own time force upon the whole human race his era
of social righteousness. There is therefore good reason to
doubt that God necessarily sides with the revolutionary, for
every last human being is accountable to God's standard
of justice and needs divine forgiveness and regeneration.
Revolution cannot in fact guarantee the common good any
more than it can guarantee a substitution of better social
structures or an avoidance of anarchy. Unless worship of
God and obedience to his commands are at the center of
social change, an overthrow of authority can even lead to
worse rather than better alternatives. Latin America has
had a long history of violence and revolution, and few lasting
solutions have emerged; one revolution continues to invite
another.

That "God speaks in revolution" is a contemporary cliché

laden with theological vulnerability. Such a claim implies
that revolution is inevitable, since it is assertedly a framework in which the voice of God is heard. But notions of
the inevitability of revolution are grounded in the teaching
of Karl Marx rather than in the teaching of Jesus of Nazareth. If God speaks in revolution, then the more vocal the
divine is, the more explosive should be the "bang." On this
basis inflammatory radicals who demand the forcible overthrow of established authority become holy prophets. If
God speaks in revolution *per se,* then the theology of revolution can, moreover, adduce no objective criterion for
distinguishing good from bad revolutions. We can no
longer consider even the bloodiest of revolutions demonic,
once revolution is assimilated to God's Word. Such radical
theory must baptize and bless even the wildest and worst
options for altering the social order in the name of the God
who speaks. But evangelical Christianity cannot accept the
dogma that revolutionary violence is the necessary midwife
of history.

To be sure, the revolutionary theologian does not always
call for military force or physical violence; today much
emphasis is instead placed on structural violence, or on
disruptive techniques to overthrow existing public agencies.
Some spokesmen even consider physical violence as intrinsically abhorrent to the Christian commitment to love. But
the logic of the revolutionary position leads to a justification
of violence "as a last resort and in extreme circumstances."
Dietrich Bonhoeffer argued that love may sometimes properly serve to motivate physical violence, for example, in a
plot to take the life of a leader like Hitler. In any event the
distinction between the forced overthrow of structures by
disruptive tactics and by physical violence is more quantita-
tive and verbal than practical and actual. *Revolution ohne
Zwang* (revolution without violence) is a delusion, as any
student of history must surely recognize; revolution is a

bloody-business, and in its crossfire there is little time for semantic subleties.

Leading evangelical evangelists, Billy Graham among them, now often refer to the gospel as the most revolutionary force in history. Agencies like Campus Crusade speak of the Jesus Revolution and appropriate the term in a regenerative and nonviolent sense, and a recent evangelical book is titled *Christ the Tiger*. But it would seem preferable to avoid any verbal umbrella that opens agreeably black or white one day but may tomorrow turn unexpectedly red. To make revolution mean only change merely confuses the issue; if one means change one ought to say so, and not create needless sympathy for revolution. Radicals bent on revolution are not likely to be impressed by a church that emphasizes how revolutionary Christianity is. Since the historic gospel runs counter to the trend of the world, they are more likely to misread such evangelical affirmations as an endorsement of their own social programs.

Whoever ventures to speak of a Christian theology of revolution, ought earnestly to ask what basis if any the New Testament offers for the follower of Jesus Christ to exert violence against duly constituted civil authority. Where in the New Testament does God approve use of the sword against injustice except in and through obedience to magisterial power? Where does the God of the New Testament utter a single endorsement of revolution as a human means or method of social change? Where does Jesus of Nazareth give his followers — even the clergy and theologians — the right to force Kingdom-structures upon the world? Periodic attempts to depict Jesus as a radical revolutionary zealot reflect not the role Jesus chose for himself, but the view of some of his Roman accusers; Matthew the tax-gatherer was as fully at home among Jesus' disciples as was Simon Zelotes. Does not even Jesus say — and this in the context of Pilate's authority — that whoever lives by the sword will die by the sword? The theology of revolution turns religion

based on the suffering Messiah and on the willing martyrdom of his followers into a religion of physical force and
military conquest, a religion less appropriate to Christian
principles than to the coercive Mohammedan imposition of
faith in Allah and of correlated socio-political structures.
While the Bible approves whatever is necessary for a just
society, it does not approve borrowing unjust world-tech-
niques to implement social betterment. Biblical theology
outlines quite other dynamisms than the church's use of
force for approximating the Kingdom of God in fallen
history.

Obedience to legitimate authority is divinely commanded,
since God has willed governmental power structures as agencies for human welfare. The endurance of social injustice
is not in all circumstances outside the realm of Christian
moral response. That love (agape) is long-suffering, makes
no demands on others, and forgives "seventy times seven,"
doubtless has little meaning for a theory of ethics oriented
only to the changing of social structures. But suffering for
Christ's sake has been integral to proclaiming and extending
the gospel not only in the apostolic past but also in modern
Korea, Indonesia and Pakistan. Not every expression of
protest need take the form of revolution. State powers
forfeit a right to moral enthusiasm and approval, and de-
serve the protest of the citizenry when they violate and
deny the express purpose for their existence. But the Christian populace fails its contemporaries if it postpones all
protest until a state becomes so corrupt that revolution
seems the only course of action.

It is sometimes replied that the exclusion of revolution
as a dynamism for social change rules out in principle the
Christian legitimacy of the American Revolution. Evangelical Protestants generally approve that historic American
demonstration of resistance to arbitrary English sovereignty,
on the premise that the divine sanction of human rights
limits the legitimate authority and power of civil govern-

ment. That is indeed the case, but it does not settle the issue in debate. Christianity's social-ethical perspectives do not ultimately derive their legitimacy from modern historical events. Revolution may in exceptional cases result in socio-political betterment, and may even be prospered in the providence of God who wills the rise and fall of rulers for a variety of reasons. But that does not necessarily establish the propriety of Christian support for revolution as a means for social change. Even where a revolution produces welcome improvements, one cannot prove that political amelioration in a given situation might not have been achieved by some alternate and preferable means, nor can he be sure that temporary gains may not be a prelude to worse alternatives. In any event, the American Revolution with its bloody aspects was surely no Sunday school picnic, and few today would insist that its end to injustices perpetuated by a British regime precluded injustices perpetuated by American traditions.

The case for revolution is most strongly addressed to evangelical Christians when intermediate options have been tried and have failed to put an end to tyrannic injustices. Can those who will not actively promote an alternative, if and when revolution seems the only remaining option for achieving it, accept the benefits of a new regime in good conscience if they do not help actively to bring it into being? The command to obey civil authority does not exempt the Christian from the moral responsibility of choosing sides in a revolutionary situation, and deciding which option he will support and in what way. Will he defend a government as still capable of promoting justice and order? Will he abandon it on the premise that its policies, long persisted in despite protracted protest, indicate its irremedial corruption?

The important issues here are the conditions under which evangelical Christians are to consider an existing government illegitimate and an alternative government legitimate, and whether evangelical refusal to promote revolution cancels out any bold Christian demand for a just alternative to flagrant injustices. Evangelical conscience will be unable to defend the legitimate authority of a civil government if and while that government commands what God forbids or forbids what God commands, and in the name of God's explicit moral requirements will then withhold obedience and prefer legal penalties to conformity. The Christian has on the basis of God's *Thou shalt not* . . . an inalienable right to disown the authority of any ruler or power structure claiming prerogatives above the will of God.

While revolution is not an approved Christian dynamism for social change, the Christian citizen — should revolution overtake his country — must then decide whether the destruction of dissenters by existing unjust powers is preferable to the overthrow of an offending government. Christians ought to welcome an alternate civil government if it enables them more fully to devote themselves publicly to the righteous requirements of a just God. Oscar Cullmann reminds us that no Old Testament text was cited more often by the first Christians than Psalm 110: "He sits at the right hand of God; all powers are subject to Him" (*The Earliest Christian Confessions*, Ch. IV; cf. *Salvation in History*, p. 306). Christian involvement in political change cannot be separated from the overarching concern of freedom to obey God unqualifiedly in the public scene. While revolution aims at overthrow of unjust institutions, Christian social action aims explicitly at obedience to the revealed will of God for man and society.

A merely revolutionary alternative to injustice is too open-ended to meet this requirement. If in a time of civil strife three revolutionary governments were successively to gain control, to which government would the Christian owe obedience? This distinction immediately pinpoints the weakness of those current theories of Christian involvement that call the church to lead protests and to counsel civil disobedience, rather than to release new creative moral and spiritual impulses in society. Christians are not the instruments of a formless future, victims of a frustrated faith and motivated by resentment, and lacking a unifying spiritual principle. While the revolutionary spirit concentrates on overthrowing existing injustices, the church concentrates rather on expounding alternatives approved by divine revelation, and on shaping a morally-sensitive society that seeks such alternatives through other means than revolution.

The church is essentially pro-Christ and not simply anti-antichrist; one antichrist, after all, can yield to another, but Christ yields to no man. Christian resistance must be predicated primarily on loyalty to the commandments of God rather than to a rival political alternative to an intolerable *status quo*. The church's primary duty in the public order is to enunciate the revealed will of God, to call man in society to the enthronement of it, and to exemplify in its own fellowship of love and righteousness the blessings of moral and spiritual obedience.

It is clear that Christian conscience cannot support a government that is deemed to be wholly corrupt, and that in such circumstances revolution becomes an unavoidable option. But can any government except an antichrist state be catalogued as totally corrupt? If the Christian casts his lot with a revolutionary alternative, he must venture this decision in good conscience, in the conviction that a new government is an imperative necessity and not merely a matter of political expedience or sagacity, and that the new power structure actually functions as a state in claiming and exercising political authority, and can make good on that claim. He is not free to join in the displacement of existing authority until a new power structure emerges to fulfill the objectives of Romans 13. No Christian can claim to be a citizen of a land, and entitled to its benefits, while he engages in terror tactics, revolt or revolution against its established government. If he supports a revolutionary alternative to unjust structures and laws, he will do so mainly by stimulating respect for the righteous will of God which an unjust society tramples, rather than by fueling impatience, resentments and revolt.

The fact that the Bible holds before man the assured prospect of a coming age of universal peace and justice provides no basis for any forcible Christian imposition of social ideals. Social activists seeking to supply a Christian basis for the theology of revolution emphasize that catastrophic judgment is integral to Biblical messianism and eschatology, and on that ground argue that revolutionary social action is basic to the dynamic nature of all God's action in history. But to transpose the end-time messianic prerogatives in this way to the church in history is sheer presumption. That the Son of God will descend at last upon the nations in cataclysmic final judgment and in power and great glory is beyond doubt. But vengeance belongs to God alone, and not to the twentieth-century avant garde.

The radical activists insist that revolutionary social action *now* is required if any hopeful future is to be preserved for mankind. But undefined utopian hopes and expectations are vulnerable to all sorts of ideological exploitation and can be filled with costly illusions. Our century has more than once seen Western man's social aspirations balloon with non-Christian content, only to burst in showers of Nazi, Fascist and Communist ideology. Instead of the perilous propaganda that God is today speaking in revolution, both church and world need to hear what God has been urgently saying for centuries and is saying still, namely, that refusal to heed his commandments and to hear the gospel of Christ is what really underlies the plight of the modern world and the ailing condition of the church. With or without social revolution, the modern world will plunge headlong into another Dark Ages of culture and civilization unless it speedily and thoroughly mends its ways to live not alone by bread that perishes but by the imperishable Word uttered by the God of creation and redemption. Where

Scriptural options and dynamisms are honored, revolution is neither necessary nor inevitable, indeed, it is neither desirable nor plausible.

Yet the revolutionary acceleration of modern history will probably become unavoidable unless Christians now bring the *status quo* under searching, searing divine scrutiny, and unless the twentieth century turns to God for holy healing. There is no need, however, to give away the future by granting to radicals who would have it thus that we already live in a revolutionary milieu; too much in the way of government and law and order still survives to hurriedly hand over contemporary history to revolutionary claimants. But without hope man's spirit dies, and today multitudes of people yearn for fresh and more promising ways of life and action.

At the heart of the Bible stands the expectation of the Kingdom of God together with the recognition that everything on earth must and will be transformed. Seen against the gospel promise and Bible pattern of a new life and a new creation the present history of mankind with its man-made pseudo-alternatives looks bleak indeed. More than all the other sources of human hope for a better day, the Hebrew vision and realization of freedom from bondage in Egypt, the prophetic promise of universal righteousness, and the Christian confidence in Christ the King of kings and Judge and Ruler of all, have nourished expectation of a coming age of world peace and justice. More indebted to this Christian missionary message than is generally recognized stands the African's dream of freedom from the colonial past, the black man's aspirations for equality in the United States, and even the Marxist confidence in a radically changed world history.

Too often has the conscience of the church despite this holy vision become sluggish over the *status quo,* so that Christians imply to the world that things must remain as they are. And not infrequently has institutional Christianity identified itself with oppressive and unjust political powers and programs. This failure to make known God's demands for a new humanity gives radical malcontents an unrivaled opportunity to challenge social wrongs in the name of inadequate, and equally objectionable alternatives, even as the sorry spectacles of church-state identification in European history unwittingly encouraged the French and Russian Revolutions. When institutional Christianity yields to identification with reactionary rather than regenerative forces, it secretly contracts its own suicide. Constrained to repudiate the reigning authority, structures and institutions in order to rid society of grievous inequities, revolutionary forces will not spare even the authority, structures and institutions of the Christian church. When the living God of the Bible is then invoked by social reconstructionists for the cause of revolution, Christians as a penalty for their social disengagement face the still worse danger of being condemned to social irrelevance.

To do nothing about social wrongs is to do the wrong thing. Simply to avoid civil disobedience is one way of needlessly giving carte blanche to radical causes. The only valid alternative to a theology of revolution is an evangelical commitment to earnest and energetic social involvement.

Personal Evangelism 6
and Social Justice

The tension between personal evangelism and social involvement is not peculiar to evangelical Christianity, nor is the welding of inner spiritual commitment to public confrontation of social injustice solely a modern problem.

To be sure, some religions and world-views escape this tension due to an even deeper difficulty, their forfeiture of social concern or of personal spiritual decision as a significant priority. Certain religions like Buddhism and Hinduism, for example, are personal religions only and have no doctrine of society. Communist ideology, on the other hand, is preoccupied solely with the forced revolutionizing of social structures, and values religion only to promote its collectivistic theory of society.

But the Biblical view declares both individual conversion and social justice to be alike indispensable. The Bible calls for personal holiness and for sweeping societal changes; it refuses to substitute private religion for social responsibility or social engagement for personal commitment to God. The Bible seeks righteousness throughout God's creation, and commands man to love God with his whole being (Matt. 22:37), to walk uprightly and to seek justice (Micah 2:7), in short, to love his neighbor as himself.

The contrast between the regeneration of man and society demanded by the Biblical revelation, and social changes projected by moral philosophers, by political reformers and by founders even of great religions is undeniable and staggering. The Bible envisages nothing less than a new man, a new society, a veritable new heaven and earth in which universal righteousness prevails.

Since man's present world is obviously imperfect, any belief in the perfecting of society must presuppose altering some of its present deficient aspects. We remember how the twentieth century was fascinated first of all by evolutionary expectations; a utopian future was to be humanly facilitated by scientific methods and democratic processes. Then came the lure of Communist theory which guaranteed a new social order through political revolution. But the Bible grapples far more realistically with the underlying fact of sin in the human will. Nowhere does it diagnose the defective element in human history simply in terms of external environment — be it the lag of an evolutionary cosmos, vestigial remnants in man of a brute ancestry, or imperfect social structures. The divine demand for repentance and the divine offer of redemptive regeneration apply and extend, moreover, even to social revolutionaries, moral philosophers, and creative scientists, and judge all their human projections of a better world adversely in the brighter light of God's own holy command and purpose. Neither evolutionary automation, nor scientific ingenuity, nor political revolution can achieve what God requires — the governing of society by his righteous command, and the etching of his divine law upon every man's heart and life.

In ancient no less than in modern times even the inheritors of revealed religion have had to struggle to avoid costly reductions of the Biblical exposition of a redeemed creation. Today Fundamentalism is often made the stock example of a Christianity narrowed mostly to personal spiritual concerns at the expense of a Christian social ethic. But some forms of Protestant liberalism, despite the prevalent impression that social sensitivity is the hallmark of liberal theology,

share this same imbalance. Besides earlier varieties of so-
called "Christian mysticism," Bultmannian existentialism
associates "new being" exclusively with man's inner response
to divine confrontation, and obscures the external reality
of the world as a necessary realm of Christian ethical engagement. And while the social gospel has become the stock
example of Christianity reduced to social action, some forms
of right-wing culture-ideology can be equally indifferent
to personal religion and God's searching judgment of all
human history.

Not even ancient Judaism or early Christianity was wholly
free of a certain tension between the personal and social
facets of Biblical faith. After the rise of the Hebrew mon-
archy, the Jews fell easy prey to the temptation of viewing
the Kingdom of God solely in socio-political terms, to the
point, at times, of excluding even their divine King. The
prophets constantly recalled the nation to the vitalities of
and necessity for personal religion. They fearlessly warned
that any separation of life in society from the prior claim of
the only true and living God would bear costly consequences,
and that defection to false gods would only deepen the
personal and social tragedies of Hebrew history; only the
living God's supremacy over man's life in the world, they
stressed, could avert social and political calamity. In the
prophetic perspective, the personal love of God is always
the determining center and dynamism of both the individual
soul and of the community that would realize the Kingdom
of God. As Jesus of Nazareth reminded Nicodemus, the
indispensable prelude to the Kingdom of God is a divine
regeneration of fallen man: "Except a man be born again,
he cannot see the Kingdom of God" (John 3:3).

Whereas Judaism's temptation was to lose the vitality of
personal religion amid the aspiration for social justice, that
of Christianity was to neglect the universal requirement
of a just society while concentrating on the necessity of
personal conversion. The Christian community was con-

scious of being a fellowship of twice-born persons, and
from the very first recognized the Risen Jesus as Lord and
Judge of all. But the social implications of regenerate
existence remained to be clarified and worked out in the
context of both the called-out church and the fallen world,
a problem far more complex than that of Hebrew theocracy.

Eric Voegelin is therefore quite right in observing that
"While the Prophets had to struggle for an understanding
of Yahwism in opposition to the concrete social order of
Israel, a long series of Christian statesmen, from St. Paul
to St. Augustine, had to struggle for an understanding of
the exigencies of world-immanent social and political order.
The Prophets had to make it clear that the political success
of Israel was no substitute for a life in obedience to divine
instructions; the Christian statesmen had to make clear that
faith in Christ was no substitute for organized government"
(*Israel and Revelation,* New Orleans: Louisiana State University Press, 1958, pp. 182 f.).

To modern man it seems strange indeed that at one time
in the distant past — before the transforming impact of revealed religion — astrological powers were thought to control
the cosmos, polytheistic gods to manipulate the course of
nature, and rulers of nations were considered incarnations
of divinity who governed by inherent divine right. Every
society, by relating its existence to some higher order or
reality whose origin and end are deemed beyond human
control, has postulated some rationale to give its existence
a special meaning both human and transcendent. This
groping toward a higher order of reality has surfaced in
many kinds of myths, not only cosmological and religious,
but also philosophical, as in modern evolutionary-gnosis.

It was the revelation of God as Creator of the cosmos and
Lord of history, and the manifestation of Jesus as ruler
over nature and as King of kings and Judge of all nations,
that purged man's misunderstanding of nature and history.
Boldly the Bible published the creative-redemptive purpose

of the world-transcendent God, who reveals himself as the
ultimate source of man and the world, and of the order of
history and society. Thus nature and history were set free
from mythological referents to assume new roles. Not by
chance did modern natural science and modern political
science originate in the Western world in the aftermath of
Christian convictions about nature and history. By these
techniques, moreover, the spiritual man in exercising dominion over the earth could, if he would, implement the
creation-mandate to realize the divine Creator's moral and
spiritual purposes. Many centuries passed, to be sure, before the implications took hold. They still remain to be
fully worked out, in fact, as and when men confess their
faith in the living God and devotion to his will, and use
technological and political techniques to promote not simply
the material aspirations of mankind but rather the moral and
spiritual goals of the Divine Ruler of the cosmos and of
the nations.

For renewed humanity, work and industry from the
Christian perspective become a consecrating of energy
and matter to the good of mankind under God. By impres-
sing the ethical aims of the Creator upon the material universe, the Christian community brings the physical world
into the service of the spiritual. Man's thoughts and plans
are dedicated in love, righteousness and hope, and in expectation of God's own final realization of his holy purpose
in creation. The elements of bread and wine brought to the
Lord's table are more than simple products of nature; they
comprise, rather, the fruit of the field and of the vine transformed by human energy. Similarly the spiritual man
aspires by mind and muscle to make human culture an
abode for the Spirit of God by extending the ethical purposes
of the Creator throughout the fallen world.

The Christian is morally bound to challenge all beliefs
and ideologies that trample man's personal dignity as a
bearer of the divine image, all forms of political and eco-

nomic practice that undercut the worth of human beings,
all social structures that discriminate in matters of legal
rights. He has every reason to confront political powers
with God's revealed will in the interest of justice in human
relationships. To participate in this public way in God's
purpose for man in the world will help erase a church
ghetto-mentality, a "holier than thou" piety that misdefines
Christian separation in terms of social isolation rather than
of distinctive involvement, and will guard the local church
from becoming a racial or class or ethnic enclave. There is
always the chance of being called "a glutton and a winebib-
ber" and "a friend of publicans and sinners," but Jesus himself gladly ran that risk without forfeiting personal purity.

The primary reason for social involvement ought not to
be an indirect evangelistic ploy, although authentic Christian
social concern will shape interest in God's justification as
well as in God's justice. But the church is strongest in the
social arena when she not only honors and champions the
right of all men to religious liberty but also disavows the
notion that men have value in earthly history only in terms
of their potential alignment with the church. Because God
is holy creator of all men and all the world, and demands
historical righteousness and social justice in all human affairs, the Christian community must proclaim his revealed
will to all mankind. As an integral part of this worldwide
community the Christian fellowship must recall men to the
high dignity of God's purpose in creation, and to the realization of his will in the cosmos and in the life of the nations.
Whether men seek redemptive refuge in the church of
Christ or not, God confronts every man with a claim to
moral obedience; social righteousness is due from and to all
men everywhere, whatever their religious response. In seeking justice in public affairs, moreover, the Christian is not
precluded from cooperation with men of other faiths or of
no faith; he ought, rather, to participate in every legitimate
method of promoting that justice.

The fact that culture and the cosmos are to be conformed to the Creator's holy will and purpose means that an all-inclusive divine claim overarches all human knowledge, belief and activity. Both in perspective and practice, the Christian is to bear witness to the divine spiritual and moral dimension in work and leisure, in learning and the arts, in family and public life. If a man's material possessions are an extension of his very personality and life, as Christian stewardship emphasizes, then evangelistic concern for the new man must concentrate not only on internal spiritual decision but also on outward material interests.

The new man and the new community called into being by the gospel of redemption anticipate the new creation as the climax toward which God is daily moving history and the cosmos. Where the church is truly the church, she mirrors that coming new society of Kingdom of God in miniature. She reflects the joy of life of a Body whose Head is the Exalted Lord himself and whose identity as future judge of all mankind has already been publicly published by his resurrection from the dead (Acts 17:31).

One need only know the history of the West or travel in most lands outside the Western hemisphere to learn how much of the modern response to human affliction has its roots in Christian compassion and motivation. Today in some countries humanistic or totalitarian agencies have largely taken over the administration of education, hospitals, and welfare programs generally; nonetheless the indebtedness of the world at large to the Biblical view of God and man for such concerns is too ineradicably a fact of history to be ignored.

The church ought not resent it if and when the world as a matter of enlightened conscience sponsors humanitarian programs, so long as totalitarian powers do not close the church's own special way of ministry to the whole man and in the interest of the whole truth. Even where welfare programs have been largely assimilated to government, and

social service agencies are controlled by secular bodies, the
church has opportunity to express her heartbeat amid human
need in times of disaster like flood, famine and earthquake,
and in a ministry to war victims and refugees. Governments
are often kept from prompt involvement because of diplo-
matic, geographic or other deterents; at any and every post
and outpost the local church can easily become Good Samaritan on-the-spot.

Modern man has largely defected from the divine culture-
mandate and the spiritual-moral loyalties within which he
is to exert his dominion over nature. No longer are scientific and political perspectives coordinated with the will of
the living God as the creator, preserver and judge of the
cosmos and the nations. Instead, the twentieth century predi-
cates its scientific and political engagements on the supposed
irrelevance if not death of God. An atheistic view of reality
readily accommodates man's scientific competence and historical freedom to the totalitarian enslavement of men and
nations. Communism propounds its scientific and political
theory on a deliberately atheistic foundation, and seeks the
revolutionary overthrow of all existing orders with almost
messianic eschatological presumptions about the final outcome of history. Secular albeit non-Communist exploitation
of nature for monetary gain likewise ignores the moral demands of a theistic world-view, by its indifference to natural
and human resources and its ready pollution of the habita-
ble earth, while scientism simply ignores the moral problems
raised by its technological pursuit of personal comfort and
pleasure.

While Christianity's overturning of the ancient myths
made possible staggering scientific progress and striking
socio-political changes, these world-spheres now pose new
problems of stupendous seriousness. Technological know-
how has given man awesome mastery in exercising power
in the cosmos and scientific discovery has impressively ex-
tended the possibilities of human life and survival. Yet

direful social disintegration and violent social upheaval characterize much of our sensate and materialistic culture. The breakdown of traditional patterns of society largely through the impact of modern scientism and socio-political life gone adrift from the revealed will of God has spawned a chaotic, frantic search for meaning in personal and group life. There are lonely millions whose life ties are severed by the depersonalizing forces of industrialization and urbanization, or whose social relationships and friendships have been annulled by searing personal circumstances; these, too, the church can bring to helpful relationships in the redemptive community. Jesus of Nazareth, friend of all discouraged and discarded people, spoke not only about the life of the religious community but also of the fate and need of the entire world. Furthermore, a technologically developing society constantly faces new frontiers of social concern; here, too, the church must lend vigilant assistance.

But Christian response can and must do more. Looking beyond a ministry to the victims of social injustice, the Christian seeks hopeful ways of remedying and eliminating the causes of that social injustice.

Why then, if redemptive religion is interested in social justice no less than in personal conversion, did the so-called Social Gospel of Protestant liberalism fuel a controversy that polarized twentieth century Protestantism into irreconcilable camps? What shaped the Fundamentalist-Modernist split of American Christianity into costly divisions from which neither the historic denominations nor their interdenominational offshoots have emerged to a happy resolution of the tensions between evangelism and social concern?

What oriented the issues in new and controversial directions was the fact that the Social Gospel compounded the historic tension between the personal and social claims by introducing extra-Biblical emphases. The church of Christ knows that the ultimate cause of unrighteousness, both personal and social, is sin. It was the obscuring of this fact and its consequences that stimulated in the Christian community a controversy over personal evangelism and social engagement provoked by those in the church's own ranks who considered social problems amenable quite independently of supernatural grace and individual conversion. The Social Gospel, in a word, abandoned a Biblical-theistic view of man and the world for a speculative-pantheistic view. The notion that the space-time universe manifests a secretly divine evolution dispensed with the need for personal regeneration. The real basis of this confidence in historical progress was not supernatural redemptive intervention, but rather universal divine immanence; the divine demand for a new birth and a new society predicated on miraculous once-for-all redemption thus became an embarrassment. The Social Gospel envisaged an earthly millennium hastened by scientific discoveries and democratic political processes in a society illumined by Jesus' trust in the fatherhood of God and the brotherhood of man. The difference between church and world was reduced to one of degree, and no room remained for any final judgment.

The liberal theological distrust of supernatural regenerative dynamisms for transforming society continues to characterize much of contemporary neo-Protestant theology. That evangelism and personal conversion have lost priority as the church's indispensable task indicates that ecumenical Christianity at its bureaucratic level is still the victim of speculative theories of world recovery. While the idealistic or pantheistic rationale of liberal theology has collapsed, the Social Gospel movement survives mainly as a political thrust. Its distinguishing feature is the confidence that alteration of social structures quite independently of evangelism can insure a new world.

Classic liberalism had relied on rational persuasion and democratic processes to implement social change; today's existentialist decline of faith in reason and persuasion, however, has substituted revolutionary force as the preferred means for gaining social change. This development continues and extends liberalism's abandonment of the Biblical insistence on internal spiritual transformation of man's sinful nature as a prerequisite for the Kingdom of God both here and hereafter. In its determination to achieve utopia by environmental changes, neo-Protestantism has had to escalate those external dynamisms whereby it hopes to achieve a just society. But because of man's wanton will, reason and persuasion have failed to yield the hoped for Kingdom. Instead of recapturing the evangelical emphasis on personal regeneration, neo-Protestant activism is turning to revolutionary social change to bring about a new world order. But surely the incarnate Son of God did not come to teach men to take up the sword for the cause of justice; rather, he offered men a new kind of life.

The modern tension between the Christian concerns of personal evangelism and social justice gained special orientation and peculiarity in another respect. Infected with Hegelian speculation Protestant liberalism not only surrendered the Biblical redemptive-regenerative view of man and the world to optimistic evolutionary expectations about the future, but also lost all transcendent and eschatological elements of the Kingdom of God. It promulgated, rather, a wholly immanent and essentially politico-economic conception of the Kingdom. The Social Gospel became readily identified with a Socialist and sometimes Communist critique of society, with espousal of a welfare state based on the political redistribution of wealth. The content of the New Covenant was thus equated with the changing sociopolitical ideals of the contemporary age. Quite in line with these objectives, an ecumenical elite demanded specific legislative and political changes in the name of the church as the bearer of a divine ethic. A cadre of ecumenical churchmen who formulated politico-economic strategy stipulated the approved content of social concern but without expounding how their prescribed legislative specifics were inherent in the revelation and command of God. Neither did they indicate why good conscience and goodwill should demand support for these particular objectives and no other. While politically-minded churchmen were busy lobbying legislative specifics in the name of the church, or of Christ and the cross, or of the Christian revelation, a harrowing famine of the Word of God settled upon the churches.

It became unmistakably clear that this liberal social ethic constituted a competitive Kingdom-ideology when certain proponents equated evangelism with political action, social concern with Socialism, and Christian compassion with political revolution. Evangelical theology recognized in this liberal philosophy, and quite correctly so, the substitution of modern *gnosis* for revealed religion. No longer are we dealing here merely with a struggle for emphasis between wholly legitimate activities to which the church needs always to be recalled. When liberal ecumenists hail the current evangelical return to world-engagement as a belated endorsement of the Social Gospel, they little understand the motivation and rationale of the evangelical commitment. The whole range of Biblical authority and authenticity was lost in the Social Gospel distortion of Christianity. Forfeited as well were the singular holiness of God, the awesome finality of divine command, the darkness and depth of human rebellion, the wonder of supernatural grace, the dependence of the church on Christ's resurrection life, and the Risen Lord's special commission to the church.

Sometimes the priority of social concern over evangelism is now adduced on the basis of Matthew 25:31-46, where the Son of Man warns against neglect of the hungry and naked and imprisoned, and emphasizes that these forms of faithful obedience separate the sheep from the goats. The passage seems to refer however, specifically to the physical needs of Christ's disciples as itinerant bearers of the gospel ("my brothers," vs. 40; cf. v. 45), and not to those of people in general. The cup of cold water given in

Jesus' name is elsewhere commended because it is proferred to one of Jesus' traveling representatives (Matt. 10:41; cf. Mark 9:41). Taken in this context, Matthew 25 would warn not against the church's insensitivity to the world's physical needs, but rather as a warning against the world's insensitivity to the needs of Christians sent to proclaim the gospel. In any event the derivation from Matthew 25 of current views that Christ is to be specially found among the poor, or that the "elect" are those who engage in social service, depends on false expositions of Christianity that violate the rest of the New Testament.

Passages like the Good Samaritan narrative ought indeed to alert Christians to the needs of all persons at their side, but they supply no comprehensive philosophy for elevating social work to priority in the ministry of the institutional church. In the New Testament, Christ the Good Neighbor is the same Christ as the Christ of the Kerygma. But contemporary versions of Christian social ethics emphasize Good Samaritan Christianity as a nonverbal witness to Christ that foregoes the proclamation of the apostolic Kerygma. The New Testament qualifies any emphasis on Christ the Good Neighbor, however, by the fact that Jesus presented himself as the promised Old Testament Messiah and divinely-sent Son; on this ground he became a center of controversy, and was ejected even by his Nazareth neighbors. So-called nonverbal proclamation, as often presented today, leaves in doubt the content of Christian proclamation, a content that the New Testament expounds in explicit kerygmatic form centering in Jesus of Nazareth incarnate, crucified, risen bodily, and returning as judge of all the earth. If the Great Commission means anything, verbal proclamation of Christ is indispensable, although this, of course, is to be demonstrated by life as well as heralded by word.

The question now frequently asked, whether evangelism or ethics, kerygma or diaconia, preaching or service, faith or works, deserves priority, erects an arbitrary dichotomy between word and deed and objectionably isolates evangelism and justice. Social action must not be viewed as an independent and detachable concern, nor may the preaching of the gospel be aborted from the whole counsel of God. Fundamental to Biblical theology is the revelation of the true and living God as the God both of justice and of justification. Only where the command of God and the grace of God are both proclaimed can the church avoid a truncated message. Where the God of justice — the God who demands righteousness in social as well as in personal life — is not proclaimed, man's height and depth of rebellion against his holy Lord is quickly obscured, and likewise the full scope of obedience to which God desires to restore him through the forgiveness of sins and new life in Christ.

The Christian doctrine of society cannot be depicted in full force apart from an emphasis on both the holy demand of God for personal righteousness and universal social justice, and God's gracious provision for a new man and a new society on the basis of redemptive grace. While the church proclaims the commandments of God in order to publish the positive elements of a just social order, she at the same time declares this divine demand not simply as a moral standard to be approximated but as an already violated righteousness requiring divine forgiveness and restoration. The church addresses the world as a world under God's wrath, and not as a society having self-capacity for healing. The church knows that only a world that hears the echo of God's command, and is kept by an uneasy conscience from its worst alternatives, can stave off social disintegration.

The church best serves this fallen world when, in sharing with the world the full counsel of God — including His revealed commands and the invitation to forgiveness and new life in Christ — she does so as having brought herself joyfully within God's will. To be sure, the church will always be less than perfect in history, and she cannot wait to be perfect before she proclaims the joys of redemption by Christ. But if sanctification is not glorification, nonetheless sanctification is more than justification, and both justification and sanctification set the church apart from the world. God's new society and the new heavens and earth are not simply the extension into eternity of an unregenerate world; rather the continuity of the new society reflects the community of redemption and its revelational commission.

The basis of hope that the church offers the world is not in science and technology, nor in political and economic structures; it lies rather in the redemptive manifestation of Jesus Christ. The church has Biblical prerogatives for proclaiming the divinely revealed standards for a just social order to the fallen world, and Christians are to seek their best realization in the life of the nations. But the church has absolutely no Biblical basis for defaulting in God's call to personal repentance and regeneration. Nor dare she obscure the truth that only a redeemed church called out of the world will escape God's wrath.

Because of man's fallen nature and hardness of heart the early Christians never anticipated earthly utopia as a derivative of external structural change in society or as an achievement of social justice attainable by unregenerate man. Evangelism is therefore all the more the church's indispensable concern. Yet nowhere does the New Testament promise a universal conversion of mankind; it proclaims, rather, that Jesus Christ will return to climax human history in awesome final judgment, including a judgment of the nations. The strategy stance of the church vis-a-vis society is not simply one of the church for the world, but of the church against the world. The church is ideally an approximate picture of what the world ought to be; the world, on the other hand, is what the church would still be were it not for the reality of grace and of restoration to divine obedience. The New Testament looks ahead to Messiah's inauguration of universal social justice at his return. But it also incorporates into its

preaching the divine demand for world righteousness, and
in no whit relaxes God's present requirement of universal
social justice. It is God's command that even now political
power should everywhere promote and sustain social justice,
peace and order (Rom. 13). Failure to do so is stark disobedience to the revealed will of God.

In many lands today political concerns are thwarted by
unstable and highly explosive crosscurrents of beliefs, ideals,
and methods, and are confused by political leaders who readily espouse utopian expectations and who for personal advancement lend themselves to popular causes more than to
principle. As government bureaucracies accumulate more
and more power, the church must witness anew that civil
authority ultimately derives from God, and that political
power is divinely ordained for the responsible and just or-
dering of society. A virile church must inevitably tangle
with powers that rule not for human justice and freedom
but for repression of the people. The very fact that the
whole human enterprise and especially every concentration
of power — whether political, economic or religious — is subject to gross misuse and perversion, increases the church's
responsibility to warn against any assumption that political
power is absolute, and to insist on its limited nature. When
government makes totalitarian claims, politics readily becomes a pseudo-religion.

But Christian duty in the social order does not stop with
warnings. The Christian prays daily, and ought to work
daily, for God's will to be done on earth, as in heaven. As
a citizen of two worlds he will engage actively wherever
possible in the struggle for social righteousness to the full
limit of personal ability and competence. Existing social
structures that frustrate human freedom and public justice
must be challenged. When the basic survival needs of mankind outrun the capacity or ability of voluntarism to meet
them, then more adequate social legislatioin may helpfully
serve the sore needs of mankind. Certain church institutions

may at a particular time in history have filled a strategic welfare role which under changed conditions could now be better accomplished in some other way; in that event to perpetuate such institutional services is more a symbol of ecclesiastical prestige and power than of indispensable ministry.

Yet Christians have sound reasons for seeking voluntary rather than legislated solutions, and for insisting on the indispensability of goodwill. The need for a new man and a new style of life beckons the church to faithful proclamation of the good news of divine forgiveness of sins and the offer of new creaturehood in Christ.

If twentieth century Christianity has not fulfilled the creation-mandate as it ought, far less has it properly fulfilled the divine evangelistic-mandate, without which the redemptive power of revealed religion is totally eclipsed. Ecumenical discussion of evangelistic versus social action tensions quickly emphasizes the social action gap in the church's emphasis on personal religion. But this way of putting the matter inverts the real ecumenical situation; it credits the conciliar movement with an evangelistic orientation which it, in fact, does not have. If anything, ecumenical Christianity, as measured by its numerous social and political involvements, has an evangelical gap.

As never before the church needs to exercise her total witness to the world in the context of the truth of revelation and of the reality of redemption. Poets, novelists, artists, secular historians, philosophers or social revolutionaries have no exclusive rights in interpreting world trends and affairs. But it is a sure Word from God that the church must proclaim if she is to merit an independent hearing. Apart from such a message, however much audibility or visibility she may command in a mass-media age, she is simply pseudo-prophetic.

Jesus was neither a social reformer nor a political activist; his message, rather, warned of apocalyptic judgment on the world. The Kerygma preached by his followers was related to this warning. For all that Christ sent his disciples into the present world as salt and light. Never do his followers serve more truly as preserving salt than when they undergird the righteousness of God, and never more truly as radiant light than when they present the gospel with joy and holy power.

Date Due